ENDORSEMENTS

This powerful, practical book shows you how to start and build a high-profit business, choose exactly the right product for you, outsell your competition, and put yourself onto the road to riches."
~BRIAN TRACY, Author of *Getting Rich Your Own Way*

If you're going into business for yourself, don't leave home without this book! With 4 start ups under our belts this book would have saved us so much time - and frustrations. (Why didn't you write this book 25 years ago?)
~ NANCY FRIEDMAN, The Telephone Doctor

The most successful salesperson ever finally tackles the issues and teaches solutions that will make startups more successful! A must read!
~ BARRY MOLTZ. Small Business Expert, Author and Radio Talk Show Host

I started my business 12 years ago. I wish I'd had *The Smart Startup* then, and I'm grateful to have it now. I've never seen such a clear and comprehensive guide for business success.
~ DEB CALVERT, author *Stop Selling & Start Leading* and *DISCOVER Questions* ® *Get You Connected*

T0160331

Tom Hopkins and Omar Periu dispel the myth that you can "build it and they will come." It takes far more than that to launch a start-up. You've got to sell your idea from morning to dusk. Inside the pages of this masterpiece, you'll get the formula for success that gives you the winning edge in the hyper-competitive marketplace.
~JEB BLOUNT, CEO of Sales Gravy and Author of *Fanatical Prospecting*

The perfect book for anyone who is thinking about becoming or already is an Entrepreneur! To prove it, go to chapter one right now...answer the questions and do the exercises! Now, run to the cashier or put it into your 'shopping cart' and check out!
~ANTHONY PARINELLO, Wall Street Journal, best-selling author. The voice of the Entrepreneur Sales and Marketing Show, Host of Selling Across America and Internet Radio Pioneer

Egghead academics and government bureaucrats have been consistently promoting the fiction that the majority of new business start-ups flounder and fail early, starved for capital. There is an entirely different kind of 'capital' that has far more governance of failure, survival or success, and my friend and colleague of more than 20 years, Tom Hopkins, and Omar Periu, have revealed its vital importance in every aspect of a business, and made clear how to get it -regardless of whether you're awash in venture capital money or bootstrapping dollar by dollar. And, since every business must periodically be reinvented or.re-started, the book is for every entrepreneur, not just the start-up entrepreneur. No one is more trustworthy on this subject than Torn Hopkins.
~ DAN S. KENNEDY, entrepreneur, strategic marketing consultant, speaker, and author of the popular *NO B.S. book series. GKIC.com.*

Plainly and simply, if you want to succeed as an entrepreneur and as a salesperson (and, if you are one, you are also the other) then you simply can't give yourself any greater advantage than by learning from these two masters! Not only have they both built massively successful businesses; they've taught countless others how to do the same. Let me put it this way: If there was just one book I could suggest to someone about to begin an entrepreneurial venture, this one would be it. Own this book and you'll have the opportunity to be guided to your own success by two of the best and proven teachers in the business.

~BOB BURG, coauthor of *The Go-Giver* and *The Go-Giver Influencer*

I have had the honor of traveling around America with Omar Periu and Tom Hopkins with the National Get Motivated Tour. And even though I had heard them before, I constantly sat in the wings and took notes when either of them were speaking. I took notes because they are two of the greatest sales experts in the world today. They have built and sold businesses for millions of dollars and have helped others to do the same! I recommend you read this book, then re-read it and learn how to sell your ideas, your products and your services like the pros...and you will grow your business, your future and most importantly, yourself!

~DR. WILLIE JOLLEY, Hall of Fame Speaker, Host of the #1 Motivation Radio Show in America on Sirius XM, and Best-Selling Author of *"A Setback Is A Setup For A Comeback"* & *"An Attitude of Excellence"*

THE SMART START UP

THE SMART START UP

$$$

FUNDAMENTAL STRATEGIES FOR BEATING THE ODDS WHEN STARTING A BUSINESS

CO-AUTHORED BY

TOM HOPKINS

AUTHOR OF
How to Master the Art of Selling™
and *When Buyers Say No*

OMAR PERIU

AUTHOR OF
The One Minute Meeting
and *Get R.E.A.L. & Get Rich*

NEW YORK

LONDON • NASHVILLE • MELBOURNE • VANCOUVER

THE SMART START UP

Fundamental Strategies for Beating the Odds When Starting a Business

© 2019 Tom Hopkins International, Inc. and Omar Periu International, Inc.

All rights reserved. No portion of this book may be reproduced, stored in a retrieval system, or transmitted in any form or by any means—electronic, mechanical, photocopy, recording, scanning, or other—except for brief quotations in critical reviews or articles, without the prior written permission of the publisher.

Published in New York, New York, by Morgan James Publishing. Morgan James is a trademark of Morgan James, LLC. www.MorganJamesPublishing.com

The Morgan James Speakers Group can bring authors to your live event. For more information or to book an event visit The Morgan James Speakers Group at www.TheMorganJamesSpeakersGroup.com.

This publication is designed to provide competent and reliable information regarding the subject matter covered. However, it is sold with the understanding that the authors and publisher are not engaged in rendering legal, financial, or other professional advice. Laws and practices vary from location to location and if legal or other expert assistance is required, the services of a professional should be sought. The authors and publisher specifically disclaim any liability that is incurred from the use or application of the contents of this book.

In accordance with the U.S. Copyright Act of 1976, the scanning, uploading, and electronic sharing of any part of this book without the permission of the co-authors is unlawful piracy of the co-authors' intellectual property. If you would like to use material from this book (other than for review purposes), prior written permission must be obtained by contacting one of the co-authors at TomHopkins@ TomHopkins.com or Omar@ OmarPeriu.com. Thank you for your support of the authors' rights.

ISBN 9781683509370 paperback
ISBN 9781683509387 eBook
Library of Congress Control Number: 2018931006

Cover and Interior Design by:
Chris Treccani
www.3dogcreative.net

In an effort to support local communities, raise awareness and funds, Morgan James Publishing donates a percentage of all book sales for the life of each book to Habitat for Humanity Peninsula and Greater Williamsburg.

Get involved today! Visit
www.MorganJamesBuilds.com

DEDICATION

TOM HOPKINS

To my beautiful and loving wife, Michele—an entrepreneur in her own right. My world is a better place with you in it.

OMAR PERIU

I dedicate this book to my daughter Alexandra and my son Maxwell for their inspiration and support in my pursuit of greatness. In memory of my wife Helen.

ACKNOWLEDGEMENTS

The authors would both like to acknowledge and thank Judy Slack, Vice President of Business Development for Tom Hopkins International, Inc. for being the glue that held this book project together—keeping the communication flowing between all parties and editing the manuscript.

Special thanks, also, to the many entrepreneurs who have relied on us for advice in launching and growing their businesses. You have done the work of implementing our strategies. Thank you for being good students of our training.

TABLE OF CONTENTS

INTRODUCTION

Even if you've started a business before, it can be tough to get a handle on all the details that are required to do so successfully. Heck, some people are even six months or longer into owning their businesses before some of the juiciest tidbits of critical information are discovered. Others find out the hard way at tax time that they should have been keeping better track of certain details right from the very first day. The purpose of this book is to keep *you* from starting your business and learning things the hard way.

Once you adopt the mindset of the novice—someone with everything to learn—you'll open your mind to ideas and strategies that can shorten your learning curve and put you on a faster track to success. That mindset alone will bring strength to your new venture. At the outset, your attitude and enthusiasm for your business will carry you far. You'll respond quickly to new information and adjust your plans rapidly. You may even be heard to say, *"It's all good"* when facing challenges because you're enjoying the learning experiences that come with them.

If you're like most new business owners, the spark, the incentive to launch your business, began with something that inspired you. Perhaps you've discovered an incredible product that you believe in 100% and want to share with others. Maybe you've been watching the meteoric rise to success of other entrepreneurs who have turned their hobbies into businesses and are thinking, *"Why not me?"* Possibly, you've finally decided to make the break from being an employee and go to work for yourself. No matter how you got to this point in your life, we thank you for including the knowledge we'll share in this book as part of your path to success.

According to *Statistic Brain Research Institute*, 36 percent of the new businesses they studied failed in the first two years. They listed the major cause as *incompetence*. Ouch! And, one of the key challenges was an underestimation of time and money commitments required to launch and sustain a viable business. The sad truth is that many of the errors that caused those failures could have been avoided. The entrepreneurs could have educated themselves better before making those commitments. With greater knowledge, we'd like to think they would have made wiser decisions, or possibly made decisions not to start those businesses at all. Making different choices could have save them a lot of grief.

On the flip side of that statistic, 64% of those new businesses were still doing okay two years later! The study doesn't tell us exactly why, but we believe it's because the business owners, those entrepreneurs who decided to venture out on their own, invested time and money, not just in their businesses, but in learning how to run successful businesses. They were willing to admit lack of knowledge and self-educate. Or, they admitted their faults and hired people with the right skills to help build and run their businesses.

Entrepreneurship isn't for everyone. Millions of people around the world are perfectly happy learning some basic skills early in life and then having their career paths dictated by the needs of the companies that hire them. And, there's nothing wrong with that. After all, if everyone wanted to be an entrepreneur, who would work in those critical jobs entrepreneurs need filled?

Our goal in this book is to help you start strong and stay strong in the early phases of growing your business. We want you to be part of the statistics for businesses that not only succeeded in their first two years but exceeded their own expectations for success. We want to help you establish a solid foundation on which to build your business to the success level of your dreams—whether it's to create a legacy for generations or to follow the "build-and-sell-it" road to success.

Within these pages, we will delve deeply into the nuances of business ownership both on the practical side, and the emotional side of things. We will help you avoid some of the most common pitfalls entrepreneurs face, keeping your ducks in a row. We'll also help you establish a compass you and the rest of your team can rely on to guide your business decisions going forward. When you have strategies in place for selling your products, handling customer service issues, hiring the best employees for your needs, and negotiating with suppliers, you'll be operating from a position of strength.

Since we don't have a crystal ball, or the ability to read one if we did have it, we won't be forecasting which industries will be the hottest in the coming decade. Your choice of product is your own. However, we will help you determine your level of commitment to that product; your ability to build and grow a business; and your management style. We want to help you determine your strengths and weaknesses early while providing advice for balancing them. While many of us enjoy riding roller coasters for fun, we don't want that type of ride for our businesses—even if we've decided to sell roller coasters!

Once you understand and start implementing the strategies in this book, you'll start looking forward to the next level of challenges in growing your business—because you'll be prepared for what's coming. You won't retreat in panic. You'll, hopefully, make wise business decisions. Sure, there are bound to be some choppy waters ahead, but you'll know how to adjust the set of your sail to make the most of the prevailing winds. Properly handled, even the biggest challenges in business can be turned to your advantage.

To your success,

Tom Hopkins & Omar Periu

CHAPTER 1

Do You Have What It Takes to Succeed?

"Don't let the noise of other's opinions drown out your own inner voice. And most important, have the courage to follow your heart and intuition. They somehow already know what you truly want to become."

– STEVE JOBS

There's a common attitude among most of today's successful entrepreneurs. In French, it would be called, *"joie de vivre."* Translated into English, it's *an exuberant enjoyment of life.* This outlook does not necessarily spring from their successes. For most, it was there first—before they became successful. Many are the kind of people who see the well-known glass half full.

1

They have strong "whys" behind their desires to step out on their own and do so joyfully. In this chapter, we'll help you determine if you have what it takes to fulfill the entrepreneurial dreams you're most excited about.

Begin by understanding that every aspect of business requires selling skills and a drive to succeed. In fact, most successful entrepreneurs are or have been successful in some type of sales situation—even if it was selling magazine subscriptions in school. They are comfortable meeting new people, enjoy competition (with themselves or with others) and have strong drives for achievement.

Are You Driven to Succeed?

How hard are you willing to work to achieve success with your idea, product, or service? This is an important question to ask yourself. Is building and succeeding in this business something that drives you? Or is it something that sounds fun to try? Growing a business requires a high level of commitment. It also requires other personal attributes.

We've analyzed the traits and characteristics of many of the founders of today's most successful startup companies. There are many. In our findings, top performers in business today are:

- Well-versed in the latest industry news and in the industry's history
- Always open to exploring new ideas and strategies
- Problem solvers
- Seekers of new knowledge that will help them grow their businesses
- Not afraid to ask for help when in need

- Self-directed
- Positive
- Rarely bored with their work
- Independent
- Unafraid to take action
- Accountable for their actions
- Willing to sacrifice today for tomorrow's success

The motivation for success as an entrepreneur is more complex than just the drive for money, achievement, power, control, or status, although each plays a role. Because of the complexity of success, it's important to identify your personal motivations for wanting to win the game of entrepreneurship. You'll want to create the vision and emotions that will keep you going on those less-than-perfect days.

What is your "why?" What will keep you going on days when you work 16 hours or longer? What will get you out of bed every morning with a desire to make things happen? Are you moving away from something you dislike? Or, are you moving toward a new and better future? Maybe it's a little of each. Invest the time to write down or take a photo of exactly what it is that will keep you going no matter what. Keep it where you'll see it many times each day.

J.K. Rowling, author of the Harry Potter books, was living on state benefits, raising her daughter as a single parent when she began writing about Harry and his wizarding world. She had always wanted to be a successful writer and her status in life at the time motivated her to move toward a new and better future. She was very motivated to move away from her current standing in life. The thought of leaving that life behind kept her going, writing and re-writing for hours on end. That thought also kept her going when the first manuscript was rejected by 12 publishers. She was driven to succeed. Are you?

Self-Analysis for Entrepreneurs

Don't be like the entrepreneurs whose businesses failed in the first two years. Do some deep analysis before you begin. If you've already launched a business, it's not too late to analyze your motivations. Just be prepared for the possibility of making a major course correction if your motives don't match where you're currently headed.

The following three questions are key:

1. Where am I?
2. Where do I want to go?
3. How do I best get there?

Let's look at some possible answers for each.

<u>Where am I now</u>? Make an honest and *unemotional* evaluation of your current position. This is where you look at your situation in black and white—no gray areas allowed. It's sort of the spreadsheet of your life—something another person could look at and evaluate without all the usual human emotions tied to it.

Are you where you want to be, or at least on the right course? The answer may be *"probably not"* or even *"heck, no."* The fact that you're reading this book tells us that you want more, that you're perhaps one of those driven individuals who feel that you *must* achieve success. Good for you! However, before you can chart your course, it's important to know your starting point.

Think of it as taking a road trip. You choose your destination but need to consider where you are starting from in order to make the necessary travel plans to get there.

<u>Where do I want to go?</u> J.K. Rowling could have stayed where she was in life and gotten by on state benefits but that wasn't her dream. She wasn't comfortable there. Her choice of destination was greater success through writing even though she never dreamed that Harry Potter would prove to be an unparalleled success and make her one of the richest women in the world.

Other notable people could have stayed where they were as well.

- Orville and Wilbur Wright ran a successful bicycle shop, but they had dreams of powered flight. Those dreams were fueled by a burning desire to win the race toward manned flight.
- Sam Walton could have been satisfied with his *Ben Franklin* "five-and-dime" store franchise, but he had the idea for *Wal-Mart* – a much broader retail store that would be able to serve the masses with both products and job opportunities.
- Bill Gates could have been satisfied with a degree from Harvard, but he dropped out to follow an even bigger dream that became *Microsoft*.

All those successful people had visions of where they wanted to be in the future.

What are your dreams for the future? Where do you want to be? What do you want to have? What do you plan to be able to say when asked what you've accomplished in your life? Think about it. Get clarity about exactly what you want to be, do, have, and achieve. Write it down so descriptively that someone else could read it and see your vision, too. Then start believing that by taking the right steps on the path to that dream you'll develop the skills and mindset it takes to achieve all of it.

How do I get there? This is your map. Entrepreneurs follow different pathways to success and you'll have to chart your own. Start thinking in terms of the steps required to get where you want to be rather than focusing solely on the big picture. Some people begin with the end in mind, then work backwards, breaking down the big picture into smaller, manageable bits and pieces that are actionable items for each day. Others begin where they are and figure out what next steps they need to take going forward to achieve small goals along the way to their larger ones. Which method feels right to you?

As an example, before inventing the airplane the Wright brothers had to design and test gliders, develop control mechanisms, learn aerodynamics, develop engines and so on. They took it one step at a time and eventually achieved their goal of powered flight. Determine the steps you need to take to achieve your goals for your business and then take them on one at a time.

Selling: The Foundation of Every Successful Business

Since we both began our careers in sales, we understand the impact selling skills have had on the amount of success we have achieved in life. We believe that knowledge of selling skills is an excellent foundation for building a successful business because you're always going to be selling something…your product, yourself, selling employees on doing their jobs well and so on. Everybody is selling or being sold to every minute of the day. That's why selling skills are so critical to overall success in life, and specific to success in business. We'll cover specific product sales strategies in great detail in chapter 7.

Some refer to selling skills as business communication skills. We like to call them *"people skills"* because selling really comes down to agreements being made between two or more people. How effectively you communicate with other people can make or break your business and your personal relationships as well.

You see, as you develop your plans for your business, you'll be selling more than your product or service. You'll be selling others on working with or for you. You may sell other people on investing in your business. You'll be selling vendors on providing their services economically to keep your overhead down. Every communication between two or more people involves selling— effectively communicating with others.

So, how good are you now at communicating with others? Do you:

- Have to repeat yourself often?

- Need to express your point in more than one way for others to understand?
- Bear the repercussions of miscommunication more often than you care to?
- Get asked to clarify what you mean?
- Find yourself getting answers from others, but not the answers to the questions you've asked?

Be honest with yourself when answering each of those questions. If you say *yes* to any of them, there's room for improvement in your ability to communicate.

Here's a scenario to demonstrate what can happen when you don't use effective people skills all the time.

Alice has been involved in business for many years. In fact, she has been a key communicator within her company for decades. People rely on her to keep them informed about happenings within the company that impact them. And, she's often complimented on how well she does this. However, in her personal life, Alice experiences frustration when family members do not fulfill their promises as she expected; forget to do something altogether; or when they go off on side tangents when she asks very specific questions.

What's the difference? It might be easy to blame the people on the other end of the communication channel. However, truly successful people will look at themselves first when miscommunications occur.

Could it be that Alice takes her business "hat" off at home and doesn't use her highly effective communication skills there? It's possible. What's more likely happening is that Alice expects since her family members know her so well, they'll understand what she means when she makes requests. This is a selling mistake! Selling requires you to be very clear in your communications—including the actions you expect others to take—no matter who it is you're communicating with.

One of Alice's biggest challenges is that she doesn't think she needs to sell herself at home. She's a person in authority in her family. She must be obeyed. She doesn't understand the concept that selling happens all the time even when you're communicating with loved ones—especially when you're selling your values to children.

If you're like Alice learn this lesson now, right here in the first chapter of this book: *You are always selling* and the better you are at it the more success you will achieve in all areas of your life: your personal relationships, and your business relationships.

When you realize that every human communication you make, whether it's verbal or in writing, is a sales presentation, you'll think and act with a specific end in mind. You will become better at clarifying the information you're sharing with others. You'll have fewer disappointments regarding your expectations of others. The clearer you communicate, the better results you'll get.

If your communication skills aren't already top-notch, you're reading the right book. By the time you finish it, you'll have learned some extremely simple, yet powerful skills that will help you in your journey toward successful entrepreneurship.

Entrepreneurship Defined

Let's get real about what entrepreneurship is all about. Defined, *an entrepreneur is a person who organizes and manages an enterprise, especially a business, usually with considerable initiative and risk.* Your authors are both entrepreneurs. We have demonstrated initiative for many years. And we're somewhat risk-tolerant. How about you? Are you risk-tolerant?

Before saying *yes* and making a commitment to a business launch, consider these questions:

- Are you comfortable taking a certain amount of risk? Or does the unknown frighten you into immobility?
- Are you confident in your ability to evaluate information and make wise decisions? And can you do so without delay?
- Do you have the skill set necessary to persuade others to either join you in your new endeavor or to sell your product/service to others?
- Can you sell yourself on keeping going on days when there seem to be more challenges than rewards?
- Do you have solid negotiation skills?
- Are you able to come up with new ideas, new strategies, and are you flexible enough to act upon them?
- Do you have a strong support group or mentors who are willing and able to provide prudent advice?

If you're feeling positive about your desire and ability to handle the potential challenges of entrepreneurship, ask yourself these questions advised by the U.S. Small Business Administration before starting a business:

1. Why am I starting a business?
2. What kind of business do I want?
3. Who is my ideal client?
4. What products or services will my business provide?
5. Am I prepared to spend the time and money needed to get my business started?
6. Where will my business be located?
7. How many employees will I need? To perform what function?
8. What types of suppliers do I need?
9. How much money do I need to get started?
10. Will I need to get a loan?
11. How soon will it take before my products or services are available?
12. How long until I start making a profit?
13. How will I set up the legal structure of my business?
14. What taxes do I need to pay?
15. What kind of insurance do I need?
16. How will I manage my business?
17. How will I advertise my business?

It's a lot to think about, isn't it? But, think about it you must if you have the desire to succeed. The information generated by answering those questions will help you make better decisions and plans for the future of your enterprise.

Once those questions are answered there are the questions about your long-term goals for the business. Are you building this business to create a legacy for generations? Is it just something you'll do until you retire? Or will you build it just large enough to sell to someone else, and move on to other things? In other words, what's your exit strategy? It's important to think about that even before you begin.

When you have a clear picture in mind of what you want to do with your business, it's time to do even more research. This time the research needs to be about your competition. Even if you have a truly innovative idea for a product or service—one that no one else is marketing—you will still be competing for the dollars your ideal clients have to spend.

Let's say you've invented a truly novel way of keeping the exterior of cars clean. Even if your product is like nothing ever created before, your clients—car owners—still only have a certain amount of discretionary income they're willing to allot to keep their cars in tip top shape, including keeping them clean. You may be competing with tire companies, mechanics, and even automotive retailers for the other doodads and services people want for their vehicles. The proof of this is all around you in the dusty, dirty, dented vehicles, and broken windshields you see every day. With people who must choose between having a clean vehicle, or having a vehicle that runs, you would lose those dollars to the competition. Don't make the mistake of thinking your competition is only car washes or vehicle detailing companies. The more you know about your market, the better decisions you can make about entering it.

S'Whot's the First Step?

One of the most effective ways to evaluate the potential for your business is to conduct a SWOT analysis. This process was developed in the 1960s by Albert Humphrey who led a research project at Stanford University on why corporate planning failed. For many, this analytical tool is the most effective, most efficient first step toward achieving your ultimate goal.

SWOT stands for:
Strengths
Weaknesses
Opportunities
Threats

The value of a SWOT analysis to the man or woman driven to success is that it quickly brings together a lot of information in an easily understood format. This information addresses the most promising opportunities and the most crucial issues (good and bad). The process takes a bit of time and effort because it's important to invest serious time and energy into thinking about and evaluating each step. However, the analysis can be an effective shortcut to success in that it helps you to crystalize your thinking and hone in on your true objectives. The analysis can become the foundation upon which you develop a real-world picture of where you are, and help you focus on the best way to proceed in achieving your ultimate goals. Once you have a handle on these opportunities and issues you're in a position to, well, handle them.

Be mercifully brief at first. Use bullet points and don't go into a lot of detail. List the key factors in each area. Use as few words as possible. Boil down your thoughts to the bare essentials of each step. What is the bottom line of each item? Identify each factor whether positive or negative so you can make an objective evaluation for use in developing a fuller plan and achieving your goals.

The key word here is *objective*. You can't afford the luxury of self-delusion. The SWOT analysis is for your eyes only at this point. No one else is looking over your shoulder, so be 100% honest with yourself. The results of this evaluation could be critical to the success of your entire business!

Once you have your bullet points written out, you can then go deeper into detail on each item. Review what you have written and then further develop your analysis. Here are some additional considerations for each area:

Strengths are internal factors. They describe positive attributes (tangible and intangible) and resources at your disposal, such as having an outgoing personality, confidence, sales experience, access to capital, knowledge of distribution channels, marketing expertise, an established customer base, and so on. Be careful not to list a "maybe" item just because it makes you feel more secure. Again, objectivity is essential.

Weaknesses are internal forces that detract from your ability to achieve and/or maintain your competitive edge. For example, weaknesses could be lack of education, little or no sales experience, poor credit, outdated technology or technological knowledge, a poor location, or possibly an inferior product or service when compared to the competition. Objectivity is equally important in conducting this analysis. Don't sugar coat a weakness because it makes you feel better or because you don't want to face that reality (that act in itself is a weakness). You can't overcome a weakness if you won't admit you have it.

Opportunities are external factors that can benefit your efforts, such as proximity to a growing market for your product or service, a technological advantage over your competitors, experience, market trends, a positive end to negative news about your industry, or an improving economy.

Threats are external factors that could have a negative impact on your goals. These could be stiff competition, a downturn in the economy, negative coverage in the news media or through social media outlets, government regulations or restrictions, new technologies rendering your product or service obsolete, or changes in consumer behavior. One more threat—sole proprietorship. If you and only you can run the business, what happens to it and any staff members you have if something unforeseen happens to you? Does it all come crashing down?

Once you have completed an honest and objective SWOT analysis, you will be in a far better position to act wisely in choosing and following the most profitable pathways to the success you seek. For example, once you have identified your weaknesses you can begin to develop effective measures to minimize or even eliminate them. When you've identified your strengths, you can begin to put them into service to achieve your goals.

Get Organized

Writer/editor/entrepreneur George Matthew Adams wrote, *"The only institutions that last a long time, do good and useful work, and are profitable, are those that are, and have been, well organized."* If you aren't already aware of the fact, realize now that much of the business world is defined by the term *"cutthroat"* and if you're to survive you have to organize not only for ongoing success and protection but for expansion and possibly conquest.

Note that your authors do not condone unethical or underhanded business practices. You don't need them to succeed. In fact, such practices have a nasty way of causing you harm in the end. But you must be prepared to face a potentially hostile environment sooner or later in business whether it's from another company such as someone infringing on your patent, or from within—a disgruntled employee.

By *conquest* we mean the achievement of your goals. You don't have to crush others underfoot in order to reach the top of your profession or industry. But you do have to be organized in order to be prepared to take on new opportunities when they arise.

Inevitably, the successful organization builds a team or teams of people to help grow the business. That's another reason to get organized. The result of being well-organized is that it helps you fill your corporate stable with thoroughbreds and win more business. Well-qualified employees like working in well-run organizations.

"Believe that you have it, and you have it."

That quote is ancient and translated from the Latin language. No one knows who first scratched it on the stone walls of ancient

Rome, but whoever it was, he or she was highly intelligent—and understood success. Belief is the key to success because everything begins with individuals believing that their ideas, their concepts, are achievable. Everything starts with you – not your product or service, or the company, or the competition, the customers or the economy. What do *you* currently believe about your product and about the potential for launching or growing a successful business around it?

The first step toward success is to program your mind for success in selling your idea for a business and your actual product. This isn't New Age drivel; it's scientific fact. Your mind can be programmed for success or failure. The best news is that you're the one who does the programming.

We've all encountered examples of negative and positive self-programming. It's often done without conscious effort. It's what we come to believe based on our experiences. Don't believe us? How many times have you heard a friend or associate say the following or something similar?

"I can't win."

"I'm not going to make it this time"

"It's no use."

"I might as well give up."

Chances are that person's attitude became a self-fulfilling prophesy. They allowed their thoughts to dwell upon those negative goals rather than seeing challenges as positive situations. Contrast that person's situation with people who program their minds with positive thoughts. They're thinking the following:

"I've got this."

"I'm going to make it come hell or high water."

"Nothing's going to stop me now."

"I'll make it happen."

People who think along those lines have programmed their minds for success. They make achievement mind-accomplished first. Then, their minds go about accomplishing those achievements. This isn't rocket science or science fiction. It's basic human biology. Our minds are very sophisticated computers. And like all computers, they work off a basic rule called GIGO: Garbage In. Garbage Out. Fill your mind with negative thoughts (garbage) and that's exactly what comes out. We prefer another take on that GIGO formula: *Greatness In. Greatness Out.*

Fill your mind with thoughts of success and out it comes! It has to because the programming demands it. As the wonderful minister and promoter of positive thinking, Dr. Norman Vincent Peale reminds us, *"When you affirm big, believe big, and pray big, big things happen."*

Visualization Realization

One of the most powerful mental tools at your disposal is the act of visualization. Call it directed daydreaming, if you will. You must see where you're going before you can get there, even if you can only see it in your mind's eye.

The South African anti-apartheid leader Nelson Mandela said, *"I am fundamentally an optimist. Whether that comes from nature or nurture, I cannot say. Part of being optimistic is keeping one's head pointed toward the sun, one's feet moving forward."* Once you have the ultimate goal for your successful business firmly set in your mind, you can't help but be an optimist looking for opportunities and moving forward with your plans.

Some believe visualization to be a grown-up version of daydreaming. Visualization is more than just ordinary daydreaming. With daydreaming, we let our thoughts wander untethered. With visualization, you do directed daydreaming. You are the director, guiding your thoughts where you want them to go. Directed daydreaming involves all the senses. You create a vision for yourself such that you see, hear, feel, smell and touch what your future success will be like. When you practice every day, using each of your senses, your new level and type of success becomes so comfortable that it's easy to overcome any fears you previously had about achieving it.

Here's an example: If your goal is to become a successful business leader don't just see yourself sitting at a big desk in a fancy office. Smell the rich leather of your chair. Feel the smooth surface of your mahogany desktop. Hear the sounds of a bustling office outside your door. Taste the special treat you allow yourself when you reach a goal (a sip of cognac, the whiff of a great cigar, a bite of expensive chocolate, the secret pleasure of a hot dog from the best street vendor in town, whatever works for you). See the world outside your office window from a commanding position. Get the picture? (Pun intended.) Make sure you get the *entire* picture. See it. Breathe it. Feel it. Smell it. Taste it.

In your world, your *"office"* might be a beach from which you can conduct your business. Whatever that ideal place is for you, invest a few minutes each day in feeling it deeply. The power of visualization is that it helps with short-term motivation, long-term vision, focusing on what is most important, and organizing your life to achieve that level of success you see in your future.

Seven Techniques for Visualization with Your Goals

Visualization is a mental challenge only if you make it one. It's really quite easy. You are probably already an expert at daydreaming. Most of us are. We're just advising you to get a bit more assertive with the process. Exert some control over it. Again, become the director of the movie you play in your mind.

Here are the steps:

1. Make sure the goal is something you really want and not just something that looks or sounds good on paper or is someone else's goal—what you believe others expect of you.
2. Goals should be compatible. Don't set a goal to work 24/7 *and* have time for loved ones.
3. Set goals for all aspects of your life – business, financial, personal, physical health, spiritual, social, educational, and so on—every aspect of life that's important to you.
4. Write your goals in the present tense using positive language – "I am," "I have," "I do"
5. Express goals in detail. Incorporate all five senses.

6. Set goals *realistically* high. Challenge yourself but don't set them so high that they're not believable.

7. Put your goals in writing.

Once you have your goals outlined clearly, the act of visualization helps to make the unreal real. It's a proven way of focusing your energies and bypassing distractions that could pull you off course. In the film *Field of Dreams*, the lead character hears a voice saying, *"If you build it, he will come."* In the real world, when you visualize something with clarity, you will make it happen.

Mission Statements

Mission statements are valuable tools both personally and for business. A business mission statement is defined by *BusinessDictionary.com* as: *A written declaration of an organization's core purpose and focus that normally remains unchanged over time. Properly crafted mission statements: (1) serve as filters to separate what is important from what is not; (2) clearly state which markets will be served and how; and (3) communicate a sense of intended direction to the entire organization.* It's important to develop your mission statement early in the life of your business. You will use it as your compass to guide you when decisions need to be made or when you are drawn off course.

As a side note, it's just as important to have a *personal* mission statement. It's defined as *a statement that provides clarity and gives you a sense of purpose.* It defines who you are and how you will live. This relates directly back to our earlier section titled *"Are You Driven to Succeed?"*

Your business mission statement is only helpful when it's based in the real world of achievement. Avoid using a boilerplate statement found online. Invest the time necessary in developing one that's specific to your intentions.

Below are a few examples from businesses that have achieved global status. Pay attention to how they're specific to those companies—not generic.

- Coca Cola Company: *"To refresh the world in mind, body and spirit. To inspire moments of optimism and happiness through our brands and actions."*
- Apple: At the time of this writing, it was: *"Apple designs Macs, the best personal computers in the world, along with OS X, iLife, iWork and professional software. Apple leads the digital music revolution with its iPods and iTunes online store."*
- Google: *"To organize the world's information and make it universally accessible and useful."*
- Nike: *"To bring inspiration and innovation to every athlete in the world."*
- Starbucks: *"To inspire and nurture the human spirit – one person, one cup and one neighborhood at a time."*
- McDonalds: *"McDonald's brand mission is to be our customers' favorite place and way to eat."*

Whenever new products are considered for development, or a new marketing campaign is undertaken everyone on the team should be able to gain clarity on whether they're hitting the mark by referring to the mission statement. That's the value of having a clear company guideline—your mission statement.

SUMMARY

Are you one of the fortunate few who are driven to succeed? Do you have the characteristics and traits of a successful entrepreneur? Is the idea of achieving some worthy goal more important than earning money, acquiring power, exercising control, or enhancing your status? Do you understand your Strengths, Weaknesses, Opportunities, and Threats? Are you ready to achieve all you can achieve and then surprise yourself by achieving even more? If you answered yes, then you have what it takes succeed. Invest time in developing your vision of the future for yourself and your company. Then, draw up your compass with a clear mission statement.

CHAPTER 2

Choosing the Right Vehicle for Your Business

"In the business world, the rearview mirror is always clearer than the windshield."

– WARREN BUFFET

Just in terms of communication, a decade or so ago who could have imagined where we'd be today? The names Jobs, Gates, Musk, Branson, Zuckerberg and others come to mind. They had the ability to visualize the future, gain the knowledge required to put the right structures in place, and the communication skills to make their futures happen. They had access to knowledge to help them choose the right vehicles for their businesses and so do you.

Opportunities and resources are all around us. We're blind to most of them until we have a need for information about or from them. As an example, you probably drive by 20 or more businesses daily that you know nothing about. Let's say one sells a wide variety of door knobs. Normally, you wouldn't even give that type of store a second glance. However, when one of your doorknobs breaks and you want to get a new one that matches the rest of those in your home, knowledge of that store now becomes relevant and important to you.

It's the same with business. When you're starting out, you may know you want to be in business, but not even know about the types of businesses available to you. There are many. Each has its own pros and cons and it's important that you figure out the best one for your needs as early as possible. It can be very costly and time consuming to change the structure once you're up and running.

We live in a time of incredible access to information and counsel from the world at large—instantly and with minimal effort. By punching in a few digits on your phone or by clicking a few keys on your keyboard or keypad you can have the information you need at your fingertips. This includes resources beyond the dreams of the most powerful pharaohs, kings, and leaders in all of history.

Knowledge is power, *when properly applied*. In this chapter, we provide a compilation of information that's readily available to entrepreneurs including the types of business models to consider, and when to seek legal advice.

Business Structures

One of the major decisions a start-up entrepreneur must make is the type of business he or she will form. By that we don't mean the type of product or service offered, but the business structure to be used to sell that product or service. It's an important decision because the type of organization determines your tax structure, your investment program, your personal and business security, and, in many cases, the quality of your sleep. Here's a sketch of the basic forms with comments as to the pros and cons of each.

A Sole Proprietorship is – you. It's a business owned by one person who does not employ a formal legal structure.

Pro: It's easy to set up and simple to manage. Instead of filing corporate income taxes you just file a Schedule "C" with your personal income taxes.

Con: You and your personal assets are exposed. If a lawsuit is filed against the sole proprietorship you and your family could lose everything.

A Partnership is a business with two or more principals acting as partners and actively involved in managing an organization.

Pro: Profits are passed through to the partners. You don't *need* a formal legal document. Caution: It's a wise idea to draw up a partnership agreement to protect both parties and lay out how you would terminate the partnership, if that ever needed to happen.

Con: Even if you didn't draw up that partnership agreement, legally you're still a full partner *and* have unlimited liability.

A Limited Liability Company (LLC) is a legal business structure where the members cannot be held *personally* liable for the company's debts or liabilities. This is the structure of choice for many small business entrepreneurs.

Pro: An LLC provides personal liability protection for each owner and pass-through profits without the requirement of paying corporate taxes.

Con: Depending upon where you live, you may be limited to a specific number of investors. Foreign investors may not be permitted.

An "S" Corporation provides personal liability and allows pass-through taxation.

Pro: Lawyers, accountants, and financial consultants are familiar with this form and can easily provide their services because it is very popular with small business.

Con: State corporation fees are required, and you can't distribute profits unequally (as you can in an LLC).

A "C" Corporation provides significant liability protection and allows the highest number of investors.

Pro: An unlimited number of people may own stock in the corporation.

Con: You will pay double taxation.

Which type of business will work best for you? That's a very individual decision and one that should be made after consultation with your attorney, tax specialist, partners (if you have them) and whoever you go to for advice.

Direct Selling is one-on-one selling to buyers. *Amway, MaryKay Cosmetics, Avon*, and *Tupperware* are well-known companies using a direct selling model. The people who do the selling for them are usually called *independent representatives, consultants,* or something similar. They are not employees with benefits. They earn only when they sell. The advantages for the entrepreneur are low cost set up and operation, little or no inventory requirements, no need for large cash reserves, and the ability to prospect, sell and service each customer and thereby establishing a relationship that can generate on-going or future sales. And, there is the support of a name brand.

Network Marketing is closely related to direct selling. Independent, non-salaried entrepreneurs distribute a company's products and earn retail profit and commissions. In network marketing, when a sale is made, the available profit from that sale is shared between you and your upline (the line of people who got into the business before you). The upline earns a small percentage on sales generated by those they have brought into the business. Usually, these upline folks will also become coaches and mentors.

Which form of business you choose is up to you and dependent only upon your goals for the business. Even when you believe you know the best form for you, seek out the advice of the people you will rely on such as your accountant or legal counsel before making a commitment. Be sure you know what you're getting into.

Location, Location, Location

Where in the world will you establish your business? Understand that if you're flexible in where you're physically based, some areas of the United States (or the world) have more favorable tax advantages over others. This was part of the reason Tony Hseih of *Zappos* moved his company from the San Francisco area to Nevada. Read his book, *Delivering Happiness*. It's a great study on the roller coaster of starting and growing a successful business.

If you require a certain type of people in your workforce, it's wise to consider where they live. Maybe it would make more sense to have your headquarters near them than to recruit them to move where you are. Of course, this assumes you'll be building a rather large business or even creating an entirely new industry.

If you'll need to deliver your products via a shipping service, it's important to take into consideration shipping rates. You might not want to open in a remote area if you'll be shipping globally. Shipping company rates are dependent on how easy it is to get your products from you to your customers. All of those things will ultimately influence the bottom line of your company.

Maybe you just need a little boutique shop in a strip mall and want it close to your home for convenience sake. That's fine. As we've said before, each business is unique and has unique needs. It's up to you, the business owner, to think through the needs of your business and your clients, or to seek out the advice of others who understand your business.

You may be planning to start your business in your garage or basement like Bill Gates and others did. Even then, you'll want to check out the HOA rules or any city ordinances for operating businesses out of homes.

SUMMARY

Do the research. Ask the questions. Give serious thought to the answers. Then, when you choose the correct business model for your needs, set it up properly.

CHAPTER 3
The Perils of Going It Alone

"Knowing yourself is the beginning of all wisdom."

- ARISTOTLE

When sailing into the uncharted waters of launching your first business, it's easy to second guess yourself. In fact, it could happen all day long. As passionate as you might be about your product and the potential for its success in the marketplace, you have to admit you don't know how to build a successful business if you've never done it before. However, there is one key ingredient to your business you do know very well and that is yourself.

No one else can truly understand your level of passion for your product. No one else can say what you will and won't do in order to succeed. That all comes from within. Because your motivation to succeed is personal, it's important to seriously evaluate your personal skills, but to also understand the perils of thinking you can do it all on your own. You may be in business *for* yourself, but probably shouldn't be in business *by* yourself if you have dreams of great success.

The Perils of Working Alone

It's not wise to think you can do it all. There's a reason for the popularity of John Donne's poem, *No Man is an Island*. We all need help to get where we want to go. The key is to understand what kind of help we need most and to seek out those who have that knowledge or those skills.

Consider Rick's story. He had a lot of experience in building and remodeling both homes and commercial properties while working for a general contractor. He had always dreamed of working for himself, so he went through the proper channels to get a contractor's license. He also acquired the necessary bond and insurance certificates that were talked about in his licensing classes.

Rick kept details of his jobs in a notebook, recording his mileage and other expenses. Receipts all went into folders for each job. He enlisted the aid of a relative to help him create flyers he could distribute in the same neighborhoods where he was already doing work, hoping to pick up additional clients in the same area. He even learned some basic sales skills and kept fairly busy his first year on his own.

Everything seemed to be going along pretty well until the end of the year. When it came time to turn everything over to the tax preparer, Rick was asked how much he had paid in estimated taxes. His answer was *"nothing."* He didn't know he had to do that.

Not having a good understanding of proper accounting practices put Rick in a perilous position when tax time came around. He thought he was making a profit as long as there was money left in his account after the business bills were paid. And, he had used most of that "profit" to pay his family's living expenses. In the end, he had a five-figure tax bill!

Had Rick done his homework on operating with a proper accounting system and a basic understanding of business taxes, he could have avoided that disaster. An accountant would have helped him understand and prepare for costs of doing business that were foreign to him. And, that same accountant would have helped him in generating profit and loss statements on each job, monthly revenue reports, and just about any other report he needed to understand the results of his efforts. This data could have helped him focus on the most profitable jobs rather than taking any job he could find.

Hopefully, you're wiser than Rick in that respect. Take advantage of as many resources as you can find (like the ones we covered in chapter 2) to start your business off on the right foot. It can take a tremendous amount of effort to get started, but it's harder to re-group and re-create necessary systems after you've launched. When you start off on the wrong foot, it's emotionally and financially difficult to take those steps backwards when you realize the error of your ways.

Starting a business can be compared to taking off in an airplane. There's a tremendous amount of preparation done before the flight crew agrees they're ready for takeoff. Then, there's the huge amount of thrust required to get the plane off the ground and to cruising altitude. Keep that image in mind as you're launching your business. There will be days when you may not have the mental or physical energy to generate that much-needed thrust. Just keep in mind that once you've taken off, the daily effort required to maintain altitude will level off. Or, at the very least, you'll be able to work with a well-trained co-pilot and crew to relieve some of the pressure on you.

Ten Steps to Making Good Decisions

Going forward, it'll be important that you become good at making decisions. We make decisions every day of our lives, hundreds of them. Some are good. Some are bad, and some are just get-along, no real consequences decisions. Boil all those decisions down to the basics and you'll find there are really only two types.

One is a decision made following a thought process.

The other is a decision that just happens—perhaps by a simple lack of deciding.

Good decisions are derived from sound thought processes. They are based on many carefully considered factors including personal values and philosophy, perceptions both real and false, an examination of all realistic options, and an ongoing reevaluation of all those steps as the decision is carried out. A decision may not be considered smart according to conventional wisdom, but it should be considered the right move according to the person making the decision.

There are ten basic steps to making good decisions. Now, you might think that ten is a lot. But before you skip this section, read through it and think about whether or not you use all of them. You may already be using most. Learning the others may now help you to make better decisions.

Mark this page. Make it a habit to refer to this list whenever a decision must be made. We'll warn you now that you'll be making a lot of them going forward!

1. Define in specific terms the decision that needs to be made. It's important to be certain that you need to make a decision in the first place. If not, don't waste valuable time on unnecessary efforts. Ask yourself if you're making the decision for the right reasons and for the right person. That would be you and not the organization, the boss, your family, society or the folks you'll meet at the family or college reunion next year. Evaluate the reason for the decision needing to be made by and for you.

2. Make a list of all the possible choices. List everything regardless of how "far out" an option may seem to be.

3. Determine if there are sources of alternatives you may have missed and get as much information as possible about them. Use every source possible: The Internet, news media, your local library, experts in the field, friends and family and so on.

4. Consider all the options. Some can be dismissed out of hand. Others, including those "far out" options may require further study.

5. Examine the options in terms of your personal values. Strike out all those that do not meet your standards. Select the one or ones that best suit your values.

6. Consider the outcomes of a decision to move forward on each of the remaining options. Allow yourself the time and space to look at the decision from different perspectives. Play the "what if" game. "What if I decide A?" "What if I choose B?" Take a look at what happens with each potential solution.

7. Narrow your options down to which of the remaining alternatives are most likely to happen. Eliminate those that are not likely to occur.

8. Decide which alternative best matches you, your values, and your goals. Although the evaluation process is practical math in approach (A plus B equals C, the decision) never ignore your gut instincts. Your subconscious is always sending messages. Take them into consideration as well.

9. Act. Don't worry. Don't hesitate. Take action. A friend facing a tough business situation once said, *"I've got to do something even if it's wrong."* If you act and your decision turns out to be a poor one, you can learn from it, then take a different action to fix it. Inaction is perhaps the worst of all decisions—letting nature take its course.

10. Evaluate the consequences of your decision as its effects progress. Adjust as necessary going forward.

Those ten simple steps make a great checklist against which to weigh all your most important decisions in business.

Where's Your Strength?

We all have certain specific strengths and weaknesses. It's important to understand yours. When you first have a great idea, or find a great product to market, it's easy to envision getting from Point A to Point B with it as a business. That's your 30,000-foot view and what inspires most people to launch their businesses. However, when you come down to earth and realize the hundreds, if not thousands of details that go into that trip from Point A to Point B is when you need to seriously consider what aspects of business you excel at and which ones you don't.

We've never met anyone who had the knowledge and physical stamina to literally 'do it all.' When starting a new business, it's important to be prepared to fulfill a lot of roles until you can hire people to handle them for you. Here are just a few positions you'll need to consider filling:

- Business owner
- Product developer
- Marketing manager
- Sales person
- Purchasing agent
- Bookkeeper
- Inventory manager
- Shipping manager
- Social media manager
- Customer service representative
- IT person
- HR person
- PR person
- Janitor

Since you're not likely to be able to do all of that well, it's incredibly important to enlist the aid of others who have skills you might be lacking. The goal is to develop your business to the point where you only do the work for which you have strengths and hire others to do the rest.

Be aware that even when you hire others to "do the rest," you will need to know enough about each position to oversee their work. You will need to be able to recognize whether each person is fulfilling their duties well and in the best interest of your business.

Do yourself a favor and hire professionals for the areas of legal advice and accounting. These people have paid the price of educating themselves on the best practices for businesses. Why risk making mistakes that could be avoided altogether? Legal and accounting are the two areas that can cause you the biggest headaches as a business owner. Go with the pros!

To find the right legal and accounting people for your situation, ask for references from friends, relatives, and business associates such as your business insurance agent. Get connected to someone they've had good experience with. You can often get an initial consultation at no charge to see if you feel comfortable trusting your new business's needs to these people. Remember, you are seeking out their expertise and the more they understand your type of business, the better they will be able to advise you.

Here is some food for thought when hiring an accountant or CPA for your business from *CPAExam.com*:

1. Define your reasons and goals for hiring an accountant or CPA. Be clear about the exact reasons you believe you need one. Do you feel you can handle bookkeeping duties and just need someone for analysis, planning, and taxes?

Or do you need someone to take your folder or shoebox of receipts and make sense of them?

2. Ask how long they've been in business and what types of businesses they currently work with.

3. Ask how they charge.

4. What is their typical response time when clients reach out to them with questions or requests?

5. What computer software do they use and recommend you to use?

6. What references can they provide from other small or new businesses they work with?

7. Do they engage in regular continuing education? (Note: Continuing education is a requirement for CPAs. Ask specifically what courses they've taken *recently*.)

When considering a business attorney, understand that you may need this person to handle some sensitive issues for you going forward. You have to feel you can build a solid relationship of trust with him or her.

Here are some questions to ask when considering hiring an attorney that will be a good fit for your business:

1. Will you personally handle my work or is there a chance it will be delegated to someone else in the firm?

2. Do you have any experience in my industry? If not, what type of experience do you have that is relevant?

3. How accessible are you when clients have questions? How long do you take to get back to them?

4. Would we have regular meetings or communications on potential business needs as we grow?

5. How do you bill?
6. How do you suggest handling typical employee challenges?
7. What's your approach to conflict resolution if and when something comes up?

When considering working with either an accountant or an attorney, pay attention to how well they communicate with you in the initial meeting. Do they speak in their own jargon or in terms you the non-accountant/non-attorney easily understand? Do they come across as being good teachers—educating you on what's being done rather than taking it all off your hands (and possibly out of your hands) and doing *"their thing?"*

Exceptions to the list of positions to fill in your new business would be made if you've chosen to become a direct marketer or get involved in network marketing. In those fields, the company you represent fulfills many of those roles. However, you will need to keep the title of salesperson. You will also need to add to your roles the following:

- Recruiter
- Manager
- Leader
- Product demonstrator

Initially, you might enlist the aid of friends or relatives, if for no other reason than to get input on your thoughts, your product, and your plan. Keep in mind the various experiences each person has had. They're only able to share thoughts and ideas with you based on *their* experiences—not necessarily from your point of view or with your enthusiasm for your product or service.

This will not be a one-sided situation. Be prepared to do something for each of those people in exchange for their help—especially if you're not initially in a position to pay for their advice. Perhaps they'll take product in trade. If they agree to trade services with you, though, be cautious about how much time you need to commit to *their* needs versus those of your own fledgling company.

Are You A "Doing" Entrepreneur or A "Managing" Entrepreneur?

Some business owners truly enjoy performing the various duties involved in running a business. They feel alive when they feel they can "do it all." We call them *"doing entrepreneurs."* They have a desire to be very hands-on in the aspects of business they enjoy most. Some even have the desire to learn how to do the work the business requires that is initially beyond their scope of knowledge.

For example, someone who created a new product might also want to write the marketing copy for it because no one knows it better. They may also want to find or create the graphics to use in marketing. Next, they may have the desire to learn how to use the email provider service they choose to create marketing messages and campaigns. This new knowledge could then draw them to learning how to engage on social media, including running ads. Following paths like this can be quite fun and keep a *"doing"* entrepreneur engaged 24/7. Caution: It may also lead to burnout. Maintaining a certain amount of balance is critical to your well-being.

Other business owners understand their strengths lie in creating the vision for the business, and then putting a team together to get the hands-on work done. These are *"managing entrepreneurs."* They usually enjoy the big picture of business, but not the intimate details. They never wanted to do it all or go it alone. These types of entrepreneurs need to be good at managing people. They must be able to sell others on their vision and on working for them.

Which type of entrepreneur are you? Once you decide, your next steps of planning how to make your business succeed should become quite clear. Either you're going to start scheduling your time extremely well, so you don't burn out while *"doing"* everything. Or, you're going to start seeking out others to get those jobs done so you can *"manage."*

Strength Through Teamwork

Escaping from the 9 to 5 rut, getting away from bosses always looking over your shoulders, and earning rewards equal to your efforts is an achievable goal for someone with the ability to sell. Being your own boss and calling your own shots is possible, but you will need the support and encouragement of others. Some will be team members within your organization and some will be people on the outside. It is said that nobody does it alone and that's certainly true in the business world. Working with the right other people dramatically increases your chances of success.

A key to selecting other people to work with is to conduct an evaluation of your own skills first. What are your strengths? Perhaps more important, in what areas are you weakest? Those most likely the main attributes you'll want in the other members of your team. Note that your team is larger than just the people you employ directly. Clients, suppliers, and mentors could be considered part of the team—people you could ask for assistance or advice.

"But I don't have the money or immediate income to support a team like that," you say. Many successful entrepreneurs started out in exactly the same circumstances. Consider using the sales skills we teach in chapter 7 to convince the prospective team members to work for *"a piece of the pie."* Offer a minority stake in your fledgling organization or a percentage of revenue generated from your initial launch. That not only secures the talent you need, but it motivates each member to work harder for your success so he or she can reap the rewards.

Two essential team members are:
1. Lead salesperson
2. Finance chief

It's essential that you employ hands-on management in these two key areas. You don't have to be the lead salesperson or the financial person yourself, but you should understand what is happening in each of these areas. A company is only as strong as its sales team. Without sales, there is no company. And, the revenue generated by the sales team needs to be managed properly by whoever is in charge of the business finances.

The Virtual Office Environment

Even if you do decide to go it alone, you'll need to take advantage of some services provided by other people. Technology today allows entrepreneurs to staff up without employing people in a traditional manner. It's called having a *virtual office*. This way of working is reshaping the way business is being done. With a virtual office, the savings in overhead expenses are obvious; you only pay for the services you need when you need them. That, alone, helps with your cash flow situation early on. And there are the added benefits of reduced or eliminated costs for office space, equipment and so on.

There are also many free services available. This is especially helpful in the early days when cash flow may be tight. Some of those services might include:

- Strategy – through an advisory board or peer group of fellow businesspeople.
- Planning – through university students enrolled in a business or MBA program.
- Publicity – through distribution of news releases online and in appropriate news outlets.
- Design templates are available within software programs that can be used for corporate stationery, business cards, and brochures.
- Public Relations – Everybody on the team becomes a corporate messenger or advocate.
- Sales – Bring on your sales team on a commission-only basis.
- Research and Development – Talk to your customers! They are the best source of information.
- Office Management – Use a virtual office system or service to manage projects.
- Information Technology – Use Open Source or web-based software for ongoing tech support.
- Production – Collaborate with others in exchange for revenue share.

- Administration and Legal – Speak directly with public officials for guidance, using business process outsourcing (BPO), and acquiring your business forms from online sources.

Take Action

Once your team is assembled it's time to act – immediately. Here is a list of ten "get moving" tasks.

1. Determine what skills and experience you need for today and in the near future.
2. Evaluate your personal skills and determine how to use them to the company's best advantage.
3. Identify the skills, abilities, knowledge, and experience you lack.
4. Determine what you have (in goods or knowledge) that can be bartered for other goods and services.
5. Develop a network of support people.
6. Find "rainmakers" – people who can create sales for you or who can make things happen for you.
7. Determine areas for outsourcing or collaboration with others who have needs similar to your own.
8. Locate any educational institution that may have interns available.
9. Use free, low cost or as-needed services.
10. Get online! Use free and/or user-friendly platforms such as WordPress, Facebook Fan Pages, and LinkedIn Company Pages until you can get a website created.

Recommended Strategies for Low- or No-Cost Services

Initially, you may be strapped for cash. Or, you may have cash, but need to be frugal about its distribution. The following is a list of business tips that can help move things along for low or no cost.

- Evaluate what you can trade for the goods and services you need.
- Ask straightforward yes/no questions when bartering services.
- Document the details of any traded services.
- Determine the most effective means of communication (email, phone, text, face-to-face)
- Evaluate what you can offer people who need or want to return to work or who are experiencing mid-life career changes such as flexible hours, part-time work, weekly payroll, work-from-home options, and so on.
- Record all feedback and information received. You never know which may turn out to be extremely important.
- Respect the abilities of your virtual staff. Don't ask them to go above and beyond without offering added reward or incentive.
- Use a spreadsheet, journal or online software to track your conversations and work delegated to various team members.
- Network the members of your team—both virtual and actual.
- Know and understand the legal aspects of working with independent contractors.

Using a Full-Service Office

A full-service office is a ready-to-work environment that is furnished, staffed, and equipped the moment you open the door and step in. It's a great option for entrepreneurs operating on tight schedules and budgets.

The benefits are many, especially for someone just starting out. For one, you don't have the expense of renting an office, office equipment and furnishings. The support staff necessary for a successful office operation is trained and in place when you're ready to move in. Instead of leasing space for long time periods, full service offices are often available for short time frames, so you only pay for the service when you need it. Additional options are available, such as meeting rooms, video-conferencing equipment, and audio-visual equipment. Other services that might be available include high-speed internet, IT assistance, photocopying, scanning, basic secretarial assistance, and some document printing options.

The entrepreneur using a full-service office doesn't pay many of the costs associated with a standard office such as utilities, association dues, or value added taxes. Your cash outlays are significantly less up front compared to leasing office space and filling it with furniture and equipment.

Perhaps the best known full-service office provider at the time of this writing is *Regus™ Office Solutions* which offers a variety of office solutions. Their offerings provide a good example of what you can do when thinking out of the box (literally out of the box) when it comes to office space.

- A Day Office can be rented for the day, half day or even by the hour.
- A Part-time Office for those who only need an office from time to time.
- A Full-time Office, which is the basic full-service office previously mentioned.
- A Virtual Office which provides a physical address, a support staff, and a limited number of hours of private office time.
- A Meeting Room for those who need a place to meet or make a presentation, but who do not require an office or office services.
- Videoconferencing services through access to the world's largest network of public access videoconference studios.
- A Business Lounge offering comfortable amenities, internet access and complimentary coffee and tea.

The Full-Service Office is a successful and growing trend and it's certainly an option worth exploring.

Necessary Skills and Experience

Don't assume you know yourself as well as you think in terms of running a business if you've never done it before. Invest some time in self-evaluation so you'll be confident in your knowledge of your strengths and weaknesses. Consider what you lack, where you can acquire the knowledge and skills you need (college, continuing education, seminars, online courses, and so on), and how and when you can learn the following: strategy, planning, budgeting, finance, marketing, sales, production, facilities, information technology, and administration.

When you reach the point where you need to bring someone else on, hire only people who are competent and highly motivated. It can be costly to your business to hire someone because they're offering their services inexpensively. Don't learn tough lessons because you got what you paid for. Put a value on the service you need. There are all sorts of online resources in blog posts, chats, or even website that provide normal and customary rates for various types of work. Do your homework before hiring. Ask: What is it worth to your business to have a particular job done very well? Then, decide what you're willing to pay for it.

Be exceptionally clear about the conditions of employment or partnership up front and don't enter into an agreement until any ambiguities are cleared up. Build on a solid foundation of shared agreement.

The Most Common Daily Challenges

In surveying some of the students of our training who are in business for themselves, we uncovered the biggest challenges they face on a daily basis. Here's a list of the most common ones we heard:

- Prioritizing correctly. Not trying to go in 20 directions at once!
- Getting motivated early in the morning or staying motivated late at night.
- Too much work, not enough time in the day.
- Maintaining balance in life.
- Staying focused on the key activities that grow and maintain the business.

Let's look at each one.

We mentioned the importance of <u>getting organized</u> in chapter 1. Once you've launched your business, it's even more important to *stay* organized. Strong organizational skills will overcome most of the challenges we heard from our students. When you're organized, you will readily see the steps that need to be taken next. You'll see the small fires that need to be put out while they're still small. You'll have a longer-range plan in place to guide your actions for each month, week, and day.

When prioritizing your activities, focus on the ones that pay the bills first—sales. When the money is coming in from sales, a lot of other worries go away. When sales are slow, every other aspect of the business is negatively impacted. If you can take the steps to generate the minimum required revenue to keep the business afloat during the first half of your month, you'll be able to focus the last two weeks on efforts that might allow you to generate that same revenue in just the first week of next month.

To start each day off motivated, keep your long-term goals highly visible. When you are constantly reminded of why you're in business, it'll be easy to keep your motivation high. If you find your goals are not motivating enough, it's time to step back for a couple of days and set new, more motivating goals. It's that simple.

When running a business, it may seem like the work is never done and that's okay. As you go along in business, you should be coming up with new ideas and strategies all the time. Just don't let them drag you around. Keep a master list of all the ideas that come to you. Plan a block of time each week to review that list.

Choose the most reasonable (or profitable) one to work into your next week's schedule. The other ideas will wait for you. You'll cross some off the list because they end up not being feasible. The really good ones will inspire you to plan the actions they require wisely.

At the very least, look at a month's time and plan it out. Don't book every minute of every day because stuff happens. Don't risk starting a domino effect of a series of challenges because one tightly-scheduled day got off-kilter. You run the risk of added stress as you play catch up trying to put everything back on schedule. That's letting the business run you, instead of you running the business.

To create balance, schedule personal activities as if they're the most important business meetings you'll ever have. Make time for those non-business activities. It's important to have a life while building a business. Otherwise, what's the point of achieving success? Too many entrepreneurs have crashed-and-burned because business became their lives. Then, when they needed the support of friends and loved ones, the support was meager because those people had been left in the dust by the entrepreneurs who were too busy to maintain personal relationships. Don't do that! No business is worth losing your health or the most important relationships in your life.

Make it a habit to ask yourself this question several times a day, *"What can be done to grow and maintain the business?"* Is it to serve existing clients better and develop them as advocates? Is it to do the work of prospecting for new clients? Or, is it to develop additional products that existing clients are seeking? Maybe it's to find more economical ways to create your products or manage the business. By constantly asking the right questions, you'll discover a variety of answers that all point in the same direction—to the greater success of your business.

SUMMARY

Operate with the understanding that "going it alone" may hinder the success of your business. Take advantage of the knowledge of others but make decisions that are *your decisions*— not someone else's. Focus on the best use of your time to maintain balance in life while building and growing your business. Knowing what you're capable of and competent to accomplish, you'll make the right decisions for your business…and yourself.

CHAPTER 4
Putting Everybody on the Sales Team

"Excellence always sells."

– Earl Nightingale

It's critical to the success of every business that each staff or team member clearly understands his or her role in the company. Having duties outlined in detail will save you a lot of hassle over the months and years of growing your business. When new people come on board, they'll be able to quickly see who does what and where they fit in with the team.

When the inevitable happens that a ball gets dropped—and it will—it will be easy to determine where and how that happened. Then, you'll rapidly be able to implement a new strategy to prevent it from happening again. Sometimes, it'll be a matter of adding an accountability step. Other times, it will require someone else on the team to provide direct supervision of the task. Great managing leaders rapidly analyze situations, are flexible in finding solutions, and make wise decisions. Another, even more important trait is that great managing leaders understand that every interaction—with a buyer, an existing client, a vendor, or an employee—is a sales presentation.

Every Interaction is a Sales Presentation

One duty, in particular, should appear at the top of the list for every position in your business. That is *"sales."* Smart business owners understand that anyone in a company who interacts with potential clients or existing clients—even with suppliers and fellow employees—is selling. They may not directly sell your products to the end users, but they are selling themselves, your brand, and your company's image in the marketplace.

Think about it. When an overly enthusiastic salesperson makes a promise the company cannot fulfill, who gets the blame from the buyer—the salesperson or the company? In most cases, it's the company that takes the hit. It's the same with customer service and every other department. Each and every person on your team represents you and your company. That's why it's critical to hire carefully and to ensure that everyone knows they're *"in sales."*

Please realize that some people will hesitate, or even cringe, at seeing *sales* as one of their duties. Many people take clerical or warehouse positions specifically because they don't want to have to sell anything. For some, the thought of selling generates feelings of tremendous anxiety or fear not unlike the well-known fear of public speaking (one of the top 10 greatest fears of human beings).

It will be important for you to help them understand the premise behind that duty. Even when out in social situations we often hear the question, *"Where do you work?"* The follow up to the answer is very often *"What type of business is that?"* Give your staff members a very clear, brief descriptive of your product or service to use.

"Why," you ask? Because you never know where your next lead for business will come from. It's happened that a brief encounter at a social gathering opened the eyes of someone to a new product, better service, or great opportunity and the business grew as a result. Nearly as often, it will happen that the person hearing the description will remember it enough to mention it to a co-worker, associate, client, or family member who then becomes a customer of yours.

Not to sound trite, but it truly is a small world. It's believed that each person knows at least 100 other people. When we pick up on a new tidbit of information about a product or service, we're likely to share it with several of the other people in our circles of acquaintance. And, those people share it in their circles and so on.

When your staff members demonstrate competence and courtesy in the course of their duties, no matter what those duties are, they're making a positive impression about your company to the world. And that positive impression gets shared like this:

- *"I had the nicest conversation with Bill over at XYZ Company."*
- *"The people over at ABC Company are super helpful. They really cared about my situation."*

- *"Boy, I had a challenge with my order at ACME and they took care of it immediately. I was really impressed with their service."*
- *"Contact Bob at General Products. He'll take good care of you."*

Each of those compliments is a referral. It's important to cultivate a culture where every interaction is handled as if it will bring 100 new clients. Every interaction with the world outside your business is a sales presentation. The sooner you understand that and get your team to act that way, the sooner your reputation will spread.

——— **$$$** ———

At Tom Hopkins International, Inc. each of our team members is required to be a product of our product—which is sales training. It doesn't matter if you work in accounting, the warehouse, or at a top executive level, you are expected to know and use the communication skills taught in our seminars, books, audios, videos and online courses.

Each employee has a list of what we call *"nasty words"* that are not to be used in business communications. We occasionally test our team on their knowledge of these words. For example, we don't refer to the *"cost"* of something. We call it the *"amount"* or *"investment."* *"Contracts"* are *"agreements"* and so on. The words we teach (and use) are intended to lessen any fears buyers have when doing business with you.

We also ask our staff to use the questioning strategies we teach in order to communicate more effectively in all business interactions. When we use the communication skills we teach, potential clients take notice of how the conversations they have with us make them feel. That interaction often lights a spark that turns those *potential* clients into *satisfied* clients.

Long-term clients who contact us recognize the strategies we use. A brief conversation with a past client can turn into a reminder to refresh their skills. It often turns into a testimonial for us as they explain to us how one strategy or another helped them to get clients involved in their products. Every interaction is a sales presentation!

$$$

And, it never hurts to have every member of your team know how to explain your product in detail and to understand what's required to fulfill orders. When you're starting out, Ken who was hired to handle bookkeeping might need to fill in answering someone else's calls during lunch or a training meeting for the rest of the staff. If he doesn't have a good working knowledge of the products and company procedures, you could lose out on taking valuable opportunities any further than Ken's interaction.

Data Makes the World Go 'Round

Another important duty for everyone on the staff is gathering contact information. Data capture is one of the most important commodities, if not THE most important, commodity in business. When every employee who interacts with other human beings outside the company (aka EVERYONE!) keeps their eyes and ears open for opportunities either for new users of your products, or new sources of leads, suppliers, and so on, the whole company wins. Capturing contact information is everyone's job. Getting that contact information to the best person to handle the contact is next.

The Biggest Challenge

One of the biggest challenges for entrepreneurs and small business owners alike is trying to do too much. We've referred to the old saying, *"No man is an island"* in a previous chapter. It comes into play here, as well. It's not wise to attempt to wear every hat in the business as we covered in the last chapter. First of all, you won't be good at all of them. Second, you'll burn yourself out quickly. There's no better infusion into a small business than hiring the right person to bring in new ideas, new skills, and excitement for the products.

Hiring Well

When you reach the point of needing to hire additional staff members, meet with those already on board even if they're just friends who are helping. Write out the bullet points of what this new person will be responsible for. Then, you'll be able to derive from that list what specific skills will be needed.

There's an old adage, *"Hire for attitude. Train for skill."* That's a great saying because hiring someone who has a bad attitude is never a good idea. However, when you're running a fledgling business, you also need to bring along people with viable skills. Don't just bring Aunt Sally on board because she used Microsoft Office in her last job. You'll need to ask exactly which programs she used and what she used them for. If the projects she has done in the past meet your needs, *then* consider bringing her on. If all she did was write letters and you need spreadsheets created, keep looking for someone with that specific experience.

It's a tough learning experience, but people who are out there looking for jobs won't always tell you the truth. Shocked? You shouldn't be. Job seekers can be desperate people and willing to tell you what you want to hear to get the job. They figure with what they do know, they'll manage to figure out the rest.

A young woman we know of interviewed well with a certain small business. The position involved marketing and since it was a small business, that would also involve doing some actual design work on brochures and such. She presented a portfolio of projects she had worked on elsewhere and the requisite letters of reference. She expressed confidence in being able to fulfill the duties at the new business. It was only after having some challenges with her ability to complete assigned tasks that it was learned that the key phrase regarding her portfolio was *"projects she had worked on."* She had not been the one doing the design work or writing the copy. She was an assistant in the department who oversaw the work but was unable to come up with the copy and designs. A lot of time, money, and energy was wasted by the rest of the team in picking up the pieces of those projects, outsourcing some of the work, and investing in another round of interviews to find the right person to fill the needs of the business. Even though references were checked, the depth of questioning to determine her skills didn't reveal this lack.

To eliminate or at least reduce your odds of hiring the wrong people, create a list of open questions to ask of each and every candidate. Open questions begin with Who, What, When, Where, Why, and How. They require thought on the part of the candidate and longer replies than simple yeses or nos.

Don't ask: *"Do you know how to use Microsoft Office?"*

Ask: *"What is your level of experience with Microsoft Word, PowerPoint, Excel, Access, Publisher? Tell us specifically how you have used them. Describe the projects that required that software."*

Of course, you'd only ask about the programs you feel are necessary to their job function. But you get the idea.

Warning: Never hire out of desperation! If you're so desperate for help or facing a deadline that could make or break your next month's sales, outsource the work to a professional agency that has experience with what you need. It could be that help is as close as the local *Kinkos*, *Staples*, or other quick print business. They're likely to have people there to help you or be able to point you to credible freelancers.

How Each Position Impacts Sales

As we've already covered, you and your team members all need to understand that selling comes first and foremost in the business. Every position impacts potential sales in some way or another. Let's review:

Accounting

Unless you have a degree in accounting, it's important to have someone directly and specifically in charge of the bookkeeping. Even if you do have an accounting degree, you should not take on 100% responsibility of the accounting functions for the business if you're also planning on managing it. There just won't be enough time.

At first, the accounting function will likely be out-sourced to a Certified Professional Accountant (CPA) who will be tasked with keeping your books according to proven accounting practices. They will track all sales, pay sales taxes to the appropriate local department of revenue, pay bills, handle payroll, and generate reports for you on just how well the business is doing.

If you choose to hire a bookkeeper internally for day-to-day accounting functions, realize that he or she represents your business when they interact with vendors and employees. This includes phone communications, emails, and physical mail. Your bookkeeper's communication skills reflect on you. If that person takes their time responding to requests, it reflects poorly on your business. If they're late paying bills or careless in providing information or reports, it reflects on you.

Let's say sales are going great and you need to expand your inventory. You go to the bank for a business loan to cover this extra inventory. In the loan process, you will likely be asked for references to vendors or suppliers you work with. When those references are checked, and it's determined that your bookkeeper sent payment in the wrong amount or paid past a due date, that impacts your ability to get the loan you want on the terms you want.

On the other side of that situation, let's say that due to a cash flow issue you had an incident where you were going to be late in taking care of an invoice that was due. When your bookkeeper has the communication skills for contacting the vendor directly, explaining the situation, and negotiating a split payment or later due date, that's to your great advantage. Then, when your bookkeeper keeps the promise that was made, even if the invoice was a bit late, you'll receive a more positive reference from that vendor when the bank calls. Your bookkeeper would have *"sold"* the fact that you're an upstanding business operation, that you are on top of things, and that you keep your promises. And, that is reflected in your potential for business growth in the eyes of the bank.

When your bookkeeper (and everyone else on the team) understands how everything he or she does reflects on the potential growth of the company, and that every interaction is a sales presentation, this will eliminate knee-jerk reactions to situations that arise. This will change his or her thought process about the job and how they, like the sales team, might earn some recognition for their actions. Recognition is one of the seven motivators of human achievement. Wise business owners capitalize on that in every department.

Super successful English businessman and investor, Richard Branson says, *"If you look after your staff, they'll look after your customers. It's that simple."* Who wouldn't want to be as successful as he is?

Human Resources

Under Human Resources duties, you'll be involved with the task of hiring, administration, and training for all other people involved in the business. This falls to you as the business owner until you grow large enough to hire someone else to do it.

Your first job with hiring and training is selling others on:

1. The value of your product in the marketplace
2. The benefits of working with you
3. Your mission statement
4. The potential for growth within the company

In other words, you're selling them on helping you achieve your dream with your business. Your goal, once you've found the top talent you can afford, is to *help them realize their dreams within yours.*

A large part of selling others to join your team involves standard sales practices. You'll want to ask a lot of questions to determine if each of these people has the skills you need. Once you determine that they do have the skills you need, your job switches to selling them on joining your team and giving your business their best efforts daily.

Here are some interview questions you might want to use:

1. *To help me understand your work experience, please tell me, what your past job duties and responsibilities were.*
2. *What were some of the things you enjoyed most about your previous jobs?*
3. *What were some of the responsibilities or tasks you found difficult or challenging?*
4. *What would you say are your biggest accomplishments so far in life?*
5. *Why did you leave your previous places of employment?*
6. *What do you see as some of the advantages to you for joining our company?*
7. *What additional education or training have you had since leaving a formal school setting?*
8. *What types of books do you like to read? What was the last book you read from beginning to end?*
9. *What do you consider to be some of your outstanding qualities?*
10. *What do you feel are some of your shortcomings?*

11. *What are your long-term goals and objectives regarding a career?*
12. *What types of situations make you nervous or uncomfortable?*

With experience, you'll come up with other questions to use that will give you answers specific to your industry or the position for which you're hiring. These questions are all designed to get your potential hire talking so you can determine if they have the experience or knowledge you need to help you grow your business. NOTE: There are employment laws around what you can and cannot ask a job candidate. Look up the latest information online before starting your interviewing process.

Purchasing

You might not think the person responsible for purchasing for your company could have a big impact on sales, but they can—just by how well they do their job. It's critical, as a business owner, to work closely with the person designated to handle purchasing to ensure they're helping you deliver the quality of product and experience you deem necessary for your business. It's not just about the numbers. It's about defining the type of quality you want your business to be known for.

Here are a few examples:

- By economizing (aka being cheap), they may purchase a lesser quality product that wears out faster than a higher quality product. This could negatively impact the experience customers have with your product. Their negative experiences, when shared, cause a decrease in referred sales or a decline in sales altogether.

- By economizing on packaging materials, a higher percentage of your shipments could arrive at their final destinations damaged. Thus, costing you in replacement products and, potentially, goodwill.
- By purchasing low quality equipment or equipment that just meets the company's needs, that equipment may soon become overloaded and break down. It may also need to be replaced at a very inopportune time—with deadlines looming or when money is tight. And the down time you experience because of this challenge could irreparably hurt the business. What if, because of having a piece of equipment overloaded you miss the deadline on a large order from a valued distributor or client?

Benjamin Franklin spoke of this situation quite eloquently in his poem titled, *For the Want of a Nail.* It goes like this:

> *For the want of a nail the shoe was lost,*
> *For the want of a shoe the horse was lost,*
> *For the want of a horse the rider was lost,*
> *For the want of a rider the battle was lost,*
> *For the want of a battle the kingdom was lost,*
> *And all for the want of a horseshoe-nail.*

You, the business owner, should set the standard for quality throughout the entire organization. The rest of the staff should be tasked with doing everything in their power to deliver that standard within the financial parameters you also set. If your expectations about the level of quality you can get for the money you're willing to invest are unreasonable, your team should point that out to you and come up with viable solutions.

Operations

A fault in many businesses is in failing to recognize the selling that happens in the warehouse or delivery system for products. These people may not interact directly with clients through the phone, email or face-to-face. However, the result of their work is what clients experience when they receive your product or initiate your service. If you primarily sell your products online, what clients see when they open the package containing their order is their first physical impression of your company. And, that first impression is created by your warehouse staff members.

You might recall something along the lines of this topic in relation to Steve Jobs and Apple products. Steve touted the value of the *"experience"* of opening the package when receiving the latest in technology from Apple, and how that experience affected customers. As much care and attention is paid to the details of packaging Apple products as to the products themselves. Anyone who has opened an Apple product anytime in the last 15 years or so can attest that Apple's packaging is elegant and reflects a thoughtfulness that most companies don't bother with. The user experience begins they moment the buyer handles the box.

By helping your operations and warehouse team members to understand the value of clients receiving the correct product, packaged in a careful way rather than haphazardly tossed into a shipping box or bag, each and every person in the shipping department becomes part of the sales team.

- When a new client sees a nicely printed Thank You note on top of everything else in the box, it matters.

- When multiple products are sent in a single shipment and a packing list is enclosed with a hand-written note from the person who packed it, it matters.
- When an invitation to speak directly with someone about customer service challenges is easy to find, it matters.

All of these points add up to greater buyer satisfaction which eventually leads to more sales.

Marketing

It used to be that people who worked in marketing did not understand that what they were doing was selling. And the line between sales and marketing was drawn in the sand. Marketers didn't want to hear from salespeople and salespeople thought marketers didn't really know what customers wanted—that their marketing efforts missed the mark. That made sales a harder job because the leads that were generated might not have been qualified to own the products. While that line in the sand might still be there in some companies, others have figured out that it's better to have sales and marketing people work collaboratively.

Salespeople are the front line. They are the point of contact between the clients and the company. They get feedback every day that smart marketers capture and analyze to make their next marketing campaign better than the last.

In a small business, it's especially helpful to gather input from everyone on the team when it comes to planning marketing strategies. Someone in the shipping department may have had a great buying experience with another company and the ideas they share about their own experiences could lead to a brainstorming session about your marketing strategies. Your purchasing agent, may have been moved by a marketing strategy used at a supplier's company, and so on. You never know where the next great idea will come from so remain open-minded and involve everyone when strategizing.

Marketing your brand across all forms of media requires a certain skillset. Being able to get your message out in a brochure is one thing, in 140 characters on Twitter is something else. However, it's all selling—selling your brand, your company image, your product, and your service.

Sales

With the sales team, your job is to sell them on selling your product or service—every day. Your primary responsibility is to provide the sales team with the information they need about the product in order to sell it. Then, you need to stay engaged with those people every day or hire a sales manager to work with them on a daily basis.

Sales is likely the area in which you will have the greatest turnover. It can be tough to put yourself out there every day by phone or in person. Rejection is the number one cause of burnout in the selling world. To counter its effects, you or your sales manager will need to constantly boost the members of your sales team with recognition for their efforts, training to overcome their failures, and rewards for their successes.

Remember, these people are the front line. They directly and personally represent your company out in the world. They need to be treated well, treated with respect, and compensated according to their efforts and achievements. Your sales team, more than any other department can make or break your company.

SUMMARY

Everybody sells! The words and actions of every member of your team impact the image of your business. Hiring wisely for productivity is important, but it's also important to hire people with positive attitudes who understand how their actions impact the whole of the company. Strong business owners understand they're selling people not only to use their products, but to work with them.

CHAPTER 5

Maximizing Your Marketing Efforts

"The aim of marketing is to know and understand customers so well the product or service fits them and sells itself."
– PETER DRUCKER

So, you have your product in mind or even in the process of being manufactured. You know what you will sell. You've chosen your type of business structure—the *how* of conducting business. Now, it's time to answer the marketing questions of When and Where.

In establishing your marketing efforts, the first question to ask is this: *"Where will we market our product?"* The super simple answer to that is, *"Where the buyers of your product are."*

Just like fishing, the amateur might seek out a nice comfortable spot to relax, perhaps leaning up against a tree, and letting their line drift where it may. The pro may walk the stream for hours—no matter how difficult the hike—to find where the fish are hanging out. The amateur wants to fish. The pro wants to *catch* fish. You want to catch buyers. So, be prepared to look long and hard to find out where they hang out.

Before beginning any marketing efforts, you will need to develop a marketing plan based on solid research. This will vary depending on your product.

For example:

- If you're offering cold brewed coffee in a retail setting, you'll want to market within a certain number of miles of your location. That's so your clients find it convenient to pick up their brews while they're out and about in their usual travel patterns—running errands and such.
- If your product is an online training course, your clients could be anywhere in the world. You would narrow your search for them by language, job title, and perhaps age. For example, younger people tend to be more receptive to online courses because they've become familiar with them through traditional education channels.

Knowing your product is one thing. Understanding who your buyers are is something different.

Who's Your Ideal Client?

It's vital that you quickly learn the demographic of your ideal clients. Try working backwards when determining your demographic. Look at your product and its benefits. Then, think about what type of person would most enjoy each of those benefits. Your demographic will reveal itself. Depending on what your product is, you might need to know the following about your potential clients:

- Where they live
- Age
- Ethnicity
- Income
- Education level
- Marital status
- Gender
- Type of employment
- Job level or title
- Decision making authority
- Living situation – Own/Rent, House/Apartment
- Transportation – Own a vehicle/Public transportation
- Own pets? What kind?
- Do they participate in social media? Which platforms?

Your product will dictate which questions you must have answered before investing any money in the creation of marketing materials or placing ads for it.

Develop Your Marketing Budget

Speaking of money, have you established a marketing budget yet? If not, please realize how critical it is to budget wisely. Your goal is to earn a strong return on your investment (ROI) for every dollar spent. Makes sense, right? Since the generation of revenue is one of the most critical elements to the success of your business, it makes sense to invest a serious amount of time in establishing your marketing plan and budget.

For new businesses, the rule of thumb is to prepare to invest 12 to 20 percent of your projected first year's gross revenue on marketing. This allows you the balance of your startup money for building and ramping up your infrastructure.

Going back to our airplane analogy in an earlier chapter, once you've reached cruising altitude, you should be able to ease back on the percentages that were required for the initial thrust. Depending on your goals for future revenue, you may be able to back off to allocating as little as 8% of your projected revenue for marketing. For new launches, it might be as high as 30%. Please note that every time you want to launch a new product or product line, you'll treat it as you did your initial startup—with a higher percentage of the budget allocated to marketing.

Under the category of marketing, you'll be investing money on the following:

- Branding
- Website
- Social media
- Advertising
- Events

Build Your Brand

Whatever you put out into the marketplace – advertising, physical brochures, social media posts, product packaging – creates an image in the mind of your potential buyers. What image do you want to create? If you're not sure, look at other brands in the marketplace.

- For perfume companies, it's all about the design of the bottles and the images of how you'll feel wearing their scents.
- For web design companies, simple images are often preferred so they look good on desktops, laptops and mobile phones.

Read up on the thoughts behind the designs for some of the world's top brands: Apple's apple, Mercedes Benz' three-pointed star, Nike's swoosh, Rolex's crown, and so on. Then, decide how you want your product to be represented in the marketplace. What image do you want people to have when they think of your product? The ideas for the right design may come to you in a flash of inspiration.

If there's no flash, consider hiring someone else to do the design for you (again, with a budget in mind). The research and thought process you've already put into your brand should help them put something together quickly and economically.

Your Website

What works and doesn't work on websites is ever-changing. Depending upon your product, you may simply need a catalog-style website where your clients can quickly search out exactly what they need like they can with Amazon or other large retailers. Or, you may need something more dramatic with great emotional appeal if your product is fragrance or a luxury service. The style of your website may be something you experiment with based on client feedback.

Creating a website isn't much of a challenge these days, even for computer illiterates. Many companies, design firms, and independent designers can do the work for you. For the budget-minded entrepreneur, some websites offer templates and other services free of charge. For example, a business associate bid out a website design recently and was given estimates of several thousand dollars. When this entrepreneur, a computer-savvy person, saw the bids she went online, found a very professional template, and set up the business website in a matter of hours and at no cost other than her time. Our associate is also able to update the site regularly.

The most important aspect of having a website is to keep your website name (the URL) simple! If you do catering of Brazilian food and are based in Phoenix, Arizona, you might want a domain name of [braziliancateringaz.com].

If your product is something entirely new or if your business name doesn't describe what you do, you may need more than one domain name and have them all directed to the same or similar information. You want to think like your potential clients. What words are they using to find your type of product online?

As an example, Tom's website is *tomhopkins.com*. Yet, for those who don't know that his name is synonymous with sales training, he has also registered the following domains:

- *salestrainingdownloads.com,*
- *sellingintoughtimes.com,*
- *financialservicessalestraining.com,*
- *besttrainingforsales.com,*
- *bestblogforsales.com,*
- *sellinganythingonline.net,*
- *bestbooksforsales.com,* and
- *whenbuyerssayno.com,* to name a few.

Omar's website is *omarperiu.com*. And for those who don't know his name, they can find him when the search out the following domains:

- *theoneminutemeeting.com,*
- *investigativeselling.com,*
- *healthywealthymind.com,*
- *successpowersummit.com,*
- *financialpowersummit.com,*
- *fromzerotowealth.com, and*
- *isuccesseducation.com.*

Regardless of which approach you take remember that the website is likely to be the first point of contact between your company and potential customers. It is essential that the site reflect your business, personality, and level of professionalism.

Some of the best practices regarding websites are to give your visitors information, keep your search options simple, and give them options for contacting you. Be sure to include every method of contact they can use and tell them what to expect with each.

Examples:

- Emails are responded to within 24 hours.
- Real people answer the phone 24/7!
- Retail hours: Monday – Saturday from 9 AM to 10 PM

A website isn't like a conversation. You can't respond to voice inflection, pauses, or the look in someone's eyes. But a website is interactive and the easier you make it for that interaction the more there will be.

The most important thing to keep in mind when creating your website is what we call *"the really big goal."* You want the visitors who click onto your website to come away knowing that you can help them with their needs as they relate to your specific business or service. You've heard this somewhere before: You want the visitors to get to know you and to like you. And that's possible online with a well-designed, customer-focused website.

Always remember that your website is representing you and your products just like a staff member does. It's always selling! Monitor how well it's doing on a regular basis and be prepared to make improvements.

Social Media

This is another area of communication that is ever-changing. It's important for most companies to have a presence on some social media platform or another. Before launching on the platforms *you* enjoy, find out if your clients do, too. There's no sense in managing a robust Facebook Fan Page if your ideal clients primarily spend time on Instagram or any other platform. Make sense?

Make your posts visually inviting and copy light. The goal is to engage emotionally. If your product has many benefits, work up a series of posts. Only cover one benefit with each post rather than trying to explain everything in a single post. Remember, engagement is the name of the game. Short and creative is how you capture views on social media. Include links with your posts that take interested parties elsewhere—website, YouTube or wherever you post additional information and opportunities to purchase your products.

Where to Advertise or Promote Your Business

If you determine that your ideal buyers spend a lot of time on social media. It's time to learn how social media advertising works—or hire someone who does. Even though most platforms offer advertising options, some of the social platforms are more challenging to master than others. In our experience, though, once you begin investing advertising dollars, you may be assigned a platform advertising specialist to help you get the most from your advertising. After all, they want you to have a win...and keep advertising with them.

Events

A great way to network and prospect for potential clients is through events—large or small. You can host them yourself or work with someone else who is hosting them. The other person should be able to provide you with an opportunity to present yourself or your product briefly to their group.

Where to do this depends on your audience. Many home owners' associations and parks and recreation departments seek out people to conduct educational events. If your product is ideal for home owners, consider starting with local HOAs. Parks and recreation departments seek out credible people to host classes of value to those in the community. Of course, the presenter has the opportunity to also explain their services and provide contact information should the attendees have an interest.

Be sure to have a clear understanding of the expectations of the event hosts before making a commitment to attend. You only want to do this if and when the audience is right for your product. To prepare your presentation, develop a simple agenda of the most important information to impart. Then, practice your delivery. It does your business no good to flub a presentation. This goes back to our premise for this whole book that every contact is a sales presentation. If you don't present well in front of a group, help someone else on your team to develop and present at these types of opportunities.

Marketing Materials

Marketing materials must deliver sales messages including calls to action. They are, in essence, part of your sales team. When we refer to *"materials,"* please know that what you use to get the message out about your product might not be something physical. Your marketing materials may consist of images, video, or text that are posted online and shared.

An important aspect of marketing is to develop a consistent style or design that becomes easily recognizable by your clients. Check out *Tommy Hilfiger, Mary Kay, Progressive,* and other popular brands to see how their marketing stays relevant and true to the brand. Then, check out your key competitors. What are they doing that appeals to your common market? Don't go stealing their copy or images but consider what you can do to create a similar appeal—or an even better one. If you don't see anything you like, extend your research to similar types of products. If you sell an intangible service to homeowners, look for marketing materials for other intangible consumer services. The point is to come up with a hook to grab your ideal clients' attention and interest enough that they take action by contacting you or purchasing online.

Targeted Email & Direct Mail Campaigns

This is an area for which it's important to watch trends. There are many experts in the world who are self-professed experts. Some are truly experts who teach and coach others on following their wisdom. Their followers may or may not have the same level of knowledge and expertise. Some will tell you that direct mail marketing is dead. Others will tell you that email marketing is a waste of time. Yet others are more than happy to help you set up both and run effective campaigns. So, you'll need to go through some trial and, possibly, error to determine what does work for your type of products and with your ideal clients. But don't get discouraged that there's not a magic answer for this area of business. Once you find what works with your clients and for your product, your marketing efforts will get dramatically easier. (Refer to the "getting an airplane off the ground" analogy from chapter 3.)

News Release Guidelines

We live in an era of information overload. We also live in an era in which the media is hungry for news to fill the enormous amount of time now devoted to news, information, and commentary. To take full advantage of this situation, consider what aspects of your start-up are newsworthy and which news channels are most important.

For example, opening a new shop, store or office or an expansion is a newsworthy item to a wide variety of viewers or readers. The invention of a new process or product or service that is industry specific may be of little news value to the general public but may be of considerable interest to readers (listeners/viewers) of industry magazines or broadcast programming.

Invest a little time on the telephone (or at least online) to determine the name and contact information for the appropriate reporter or editor for your release. Getting the right information into the right hands is half the PR battle.

Avoid exaggerations. Don't distribute releases to news outlets that are not appropriate for your information. Editors automatically toss such materials. If they see your name or organization on too many fluff pieces they'll automatically toss your materials on sight. A relevant news release could be passed over due to your earlier misguided efforts.

Here are a few basic guidelines to help see that your news release ends up on the front page instead of that round file.

First don't call it a *"press release."* It's a *"news release."* As a radio newsman once said, *"I don't like the term 'press release.' I'm in radio. I don't have a press."*

Second, remember that the audience for your message doesn't have the information base you, or your associates have. They don't know what you know. This is especially important when there are industry specific terms used to describe your offering. A headline or phrase that is absolutely brilliant to you and your colleagues may go right over the heads of your readers or listeners. You could lose your audience before they finish reading the headline. Think always in terms of your audience and what they need to know to make sense of the information you're providing.

Point three is the basic building block of a news release – the inverted pyramid. This is a form of writing in which you place the most important item at the top of the release. Write the rest of the material in descending order of importance. Do not try to build up to your main point.

Fourth, the feature-benefit-proof rule of sales applies to public relations. "Construction of our new covered parking area *(feature)* will provide comfortable entry during inclement weather *(benefit)* to our west wing employees, announced V.P. of Operations John Smith." *(proof)* Proof can be in the form of a quote from a knowledgeable person, a study, a report or some similar validation. Without proof, your release is just a claim.

Below is a news release example.

———————————— **$$$** ————————————

LETTERHEAD

DATE

FOR IMMEDIATE RELEASE:

FROM APPS TO APPLIANCES ONE-STOP INTERNET SHOP
GETS CONSUMERS ON THE GO IN SOUTH VILLAGE

One-Stop Internet Shop opens Monday 8 a.m. at its new location in South Village Shopping Center, says owner and manager Josephine Franchise.

"Computer and mobile device consumers are busy people. We help streamline their day by providing everything an Internet user could possibly need in one location," Franchise says.

One-Stop Internet Shop features hardware and software most in demand for small business and individual and family users. "We have four experienced salespeople who have all been trained under my direct supervision at our uptown facility. Our people know the products and, more important, we know how to match the right products with people," Franchise says.

One-Stop Internet Shop opened in 2015 and earned the Consumer's Friend Award in 2016 from the *Internet Shopper's Guide*, a national publication for the Internet industry.

"Pardon the pun, but we welcome browsers. Our staff is always available to answer questions and provide whatever information we can," Franchise says.

#

Contact:

$$$

Affiliate Programs

Affiliate programs, also known as associate programs, are arrangements in which you would pay others to market your products by sending buyers to your site from theirs. Affiliate software allows you to set these marketers up with custom links that you can then track back specifically to their efforts.

Once a month, or when a certain dollar amount is owed, you would send a report and money to the affiliate with their share of the sales revenue. Many online shopping carts offer affiliate programming options. Once you're up and running, this could be a nice way to add an additional sales force without having to put a separate sales team on the payroll.

Research Potential Clients Online

There are numerous search engines to help you with that. Google is one example. As you read this some search engines will have fallen away, and others will have taken their place. The important thing for you is that there are and will always be ways to quickly and easily access the information you need.

For example, suppose you wanted to do business in Milan, Italy, but knew nothing of the city or its business environment. A quick search just revealed among other things the following topics: city map, top ten hotels, doing business in Milan, top ten restaurants, history of the city, business schools, business regulations, government bureaus and departments – and that was just on the first page. You could quickly become an expert on the topic of your choice without ever leaving the comfort of your office chair.

Many business directories are online. These guides include sources that primarily list only names and contact information, and other that provide an amazing amount of detail about organizations, their products or services, and the personnel involved in making the company run. If you need to find the right contact in an organization, you can probably find it listed online. Beyond that, you can research that person on a business and personal level through social media channels.

The bottom line to all this is basic: whatever information you need to succeed is likely to be found online and easily available to you right now.

Communicate Online

Communication is (or should be) a two-way street. You communicate with your potential clients and existing ones, but you also want them to communicate back. Email and chat services are fast, reliable, easy and relatively inexpensive. Just type a message, tap a key, and your message is instantly carried down the hall, across town, or around the world. One of the fringe benefits of email is that people often respond rapidly simply because it is so easy to do so. There's something about email that compels people to hit "reply."

When sending email or when using a chat function, be friendly, brief, and specific. Time today is a more precious commodity than ever. Respect it.

Unsolicited and unwanted emails (spam) are as welcome as a salesman with bad breath cluttering up your desk with a lot of ragged samples of goods you have no intention of buying. Don't make the mistake of trying to sell in every email. When buyers or clients send requests for information, yes, those are selling opportunities, but keep the answers to their questions as the main focus. Be sure to end your messages with questions that keep the conversation going, an offer to answer their questions on a call, or a simple call to action, *"Click here to order now."* Email is a terrific tool for setting up face-to-face meetings where you will close that sale.

If you are new to the online communication and do not yet understand proper "netiquette," invest some time looking up the proper ways to handle yourself. For example, IF YOU USE ALL CAPS, you may achieve the goal of getting someone's attention. However, using all caps is poor netiquette because it equates to SHOUTING. How well do you respond to someone shouting in your face? Courtesy and common sense are as important online as they are anywhere else.

Basically, you'll do fine if you are polite, get to the point quickly, and respect the contact person and his or her time.

Internet Promotion

An organization without a web presence is not a serious business. Lack of a web presence will likely create doubt about your credibility. Searching the web is a quick way for potential clients to check you out. It's most people's go-to for quick background checks that you're a real business and that there are no scam complaints or negative press about you. It's important to stay on top of any negative remarks about your business or product. Resolve customer service issues quickly, and clear up misunderstandings. Request permission to add client testimonials to your website to help new clients feel comfortable.

One of the key rules is to keep your new website new – keep posting new information so buyers and clients will return again and again to see what's up. Each visit gives you an opportunity to provide more information, more motivation, and to encourage more inquiries and sales. It's the magic of the two-way street at work. Post advanced notice of special offerings, information on new products, new personnel and other notices. The more clients can get to know you, the more comfortable they will be in remaining happy clients.

Privacy has always been important to potential clients and existing ones. It's doubly important online because there has been so much abuse of it. People are reluctant to sign up for a newsletter or free download if they think their contact information will be sold or rented. Reassure your visitors who sign on that the list, just like the relationship, is sacred and will not be violated. And then honor that commitment, even if another company offers you a lot of money for the data. Integrity is everything.

Another benefit associated with the speed of this two-way street is that you can get instant feedback. If there's a challenge, you'll hear about it right away. Speed is good. The sooner you know about an unhappy client's situation, the sooner you can address it. The sooner you know of an opportunity, the sooner you can jump on it.

Five Principles of Internet Business

It's easy to put up a website and then forget all about it. That's like printing a company brochure and then keeping all the copies in the storeroom. The web presence itself is essential, but as with everything else, to make it work you must do your part

1. Put your web address on everything that goes out into the world: letterhead, emails, business cards, advertising materials, invoices and so on.
2. Provide valuable and timely information to the people logging on to your site. Offer information so you can receive inquiries and orders.
3. Build trust with those who trust you with their names and contact information. Remember that people are in a hurry for your information. Don't overload your site with graphics that require a lot of time to download or are so cluttered as to be confusing. Make navigating your site as easy as possible. Don't fill it with useless information. Padding a site just for image puts barriers between you and the people you want to engage. Make sure the site is secure and that the readers know it is secure.
4. Respond respectfully. When someone asks for information, provide it. But also ask permission to provide more information at a later date. Encourage clients to share general information you send out. Build your mailing list.
5. Find and develop your niche. Everyone is equal online provided you use your resources wisely. Big organizations have no advantage over small organizations or single entrepreneurs when it comes to intelligence, dedication and persistence. You have a niche and the Internet is so

precise that you can find and market directly to those who need your product most.

Tips for Setting Up a Web Page

You can find lots of information on how to do this online, at your library, at the local community college or from your 15-year-old nephew. These are just a few guidelines to help you work with those people and other resources so the site you get is the site you want.

Design your website with the needs of your clients in mind. Do everything you can to make the site easy to navigate, and easy to understand. Make the visit to your site a pleasure, not a hassle.

Provide real information. People are desperate for legitimate information. They resent fluff and padding. Use as many pages as you need, but not one page more. The number of pages is irrelevant provided each one provides the information buyers want.

Make the site easy to navigate. Yes, we just wrote that, but it bears repeating. Three fourths of all people who bail out of a site leave because of they can't easily find what they want.

Answer the following questions before setting up your site.

1. What is our core message?
2. What is the purpose of the site?
3. What do potential clients want from such a site?
4. What are our goals and benchmarks for the site? (Specific not general)

5. How do we measure success in reaching goals and benchmarks?
6. Who is our market?
7. Where is our market geographically?
8. What sites does our market traditionally visit?
9. How do we stack up in comparison?
10. What's happening in our market?
11. What are the market trends for the next year? Ten years?
12. How can we keep visitors coming back to the site?
13. Should we build the site ourselves or hire professionals?
14. Can visitors navigate the site quickly and easily?
15. Have we budgeted enough for the job?
16. How are we going to monitor ongoing success and need for change?

Canadian philosopher, Marshall McLuhan, made the great observation that *"the medium is the message."* He explained, *"... because it is the medium that shapes and controls the search and form of human associations and actions."* His words apply to the world of the entrepreneur. Used properly, the research and analysis can shape and control the success of your own associations and actions and the ultimate success of your organization.

SUMMARY

Your ability to market your product or service will make or break your business. As we mentioned earlier if there are no sales, there is no business. And, what works today may not work next week. It's critical to pay attention to how others in your field or industry are changing their efforts, and to get constant feedback from your satisfied clients.

CHAPTER 6
Communication Strategies

*Take advantage of every opportunity to practice your
communication skills so that when important occasions arise,
you will have the gift, the style, the sharpness, the clarity, and the
emotions to affect other people.*

– JIM ROHN

Companies experience growing pains just like children do. With children, the growing pains are usually concentrated in muscles that are stretching to adapt to the rate of growth of bones and joints. With companies, it's usually a case where growth in sales requires everything else to increase—skills, inventory, space, technology, budgets, and staff—to support the larger business demands. With proper knowledge, you can be pre-emptive about your company's needs and lessen the pain of growth and change. By paying close attention to the personalities of the people you bring on during your expansion, you'll learn how to adapt your communication style, and hopefully, avoid painful blunders made by other startups.

An example of this is the ride-sharing company Uber. They went from a startup to a $70 billion enterprise, then a public company in a short period of time. Then it's controlling shareholder made what some would call errors in judgment that led to him stepping back from an executive position. The bigger you grow your company, the more scrutiny it will be under by outsiders. Your skills as a communicator need to grow as you speak with a broader spectrum of interested parties.

Effective communication is one of the biggest challenges during a growth phase—orders get delayed or mishandled, buyers complain, and your team becomes frustrated. You'll be frustrated, too. Even when you anticipate growth and think you're financially prepared for it, all the little details related to riding a wave of change can be quite challenging. Using good communication skills with your team is especially crucial during such times.

The default position for most people during challenging times is obvious: Stress. Some people just aren't very flexible, usually because they've had bad past experiences when change was forced upon them. Others want to do a good job no matter what's happening, and they see the required changes as challenges. A business owner's job is to communicate clearly and concisely with everyone in order to keep the business running as smoothly as possible during periods of growth or major change.

Think Differently about Meetings

To get and keep everyone on the same page with regard to growing the business while keeping clients happy can require a lot of meetings: planning meetings with your key employees; big picture meetings with the whole company; department meetings; and meetings with individual team members about what they need to do their jobs to the best of their abilities. They don't all have to be in-person meetings. Take advantage of the most effective and efficient means of getting and sharing the information that needs to be shared, such as:

- Phone conferences
- Video conferencing
- Webinars
- Group email correspondence
- Individual email or text communication
- Project management software

Don't worry that all your time will be spent in meetings. Many of these meetings will lead to the valuable knowledge you need to grow the business wisely. Some of the meetings may only take a few minutes. Few of the meetings will require everyone to attend. If you're organized and prepared all meetings will be profitable.

If you're using a technological means for a meeting, request that everyone sign in, log in or otherwise be on the call and prepared to start at least five minutes before the time of the meeting. Nothing drags a teleconference or video conference down faster than having one or more members delay the meeting start due to technological challenges.

When the subject being covered requires a handout, send it at least 30 minutes in advance of the meeting so everyone will have time to access it. If you're using a slide presentation online during a webinar or video conference, it's helpful to send the slides as a PDF document (or similar) so as the attendees follow along, they can make notes.

Be Considerate of Employee Time

Time spent in meetings is time away from other job responsibilities. If Bob's position in the company requires a full 40 hours a week to fulfill his duties, what happens when he needs to be involved in weekly planning meetings? Initially, it's likely the lower priority tasks that Bob handles will not get done—that is if he's a wise manager of his time. It may be up to you to help reorganize various staff members' duties to assist with planning and implementing the new strategies. Maybe some of Bob's duties will need to be re-assigned to someone else—either temporarily or permanently depending on your growth situation.

Managing change can be compared to standing dominoes. When one moves, it impacts all the rest in the line. Just beware of asking Bob to give up one of his favorite tasks to allow time to work on future plans without demonstrating appreciation for his contributions to those future plans.

Be sure to be open about the purpose of each meeting and its goals. Consider posting an agenda or outline for each meeting in advance. You don't have to list every detail of the meeting. An overview of the topic should suffice.

There are two major reasons for implementing this practice:

1. You want to benefit from the knowledge anyone on the team has on your topic and invite them to share that knowledge, especially during a time of growth. You may not know that "Warehouse Jo" (or "Joe") who doesn't hold a management position, has been taking software development courses. She may have valuable skills that could save you from hiring an outside source. And if Jo uses your computer software every day, she will have tremendous insight as to what really needs to be changed as the business grows—more so than someone who doesn't use your systems often. If Jo doesn't know the topic under discussion in advance, she might not even think to speak up about her knowledge and skills.

2. You don't want your team members suspecting that there are ulterior motives to your meetings or that there's something going on behind the scenes that might negatively impact them. It's sad, but true, that when suspicions arise, they are rarely positive. People don't think, *"Ooh, the department heads are meeting a lot these days. I hope it means we're all getting raises."* They're more likely to think, *"I wonder what changes they're putting together and how much more work they'll expect from me."* Or, worse, *"With the company growing, I wonder if they'll replace me with someone with more skills."*

Posting a public agenda goes a long way toward eliminating or at least decreasing the amount of time and mental effort spent on speculation so the work that needs to be done continues to flow smoothly.

The Power of Agendas

Wise owners and managers understand the power of outlines and agendas. Using them helps you to focus everyone's energy and creativity for the greatest benefit of the business. When you have outlined what you believe needs to happen to manage your growth spurt, it's time to share it with key individuals in the business.

Beware of assuming you know enough of the intricate details of how the people in the company handle their jobs to create a complete list. As a wise owner or manager, you'll be the "big picture" person, and have other people handle the nitty gritty details of how things get done. Micromanaging kills creativity and you need all the creativity you can get when your business is growing.

$$\$\$\$$$

We know of a company that inspired creativity by putting a twist on the iconic "Suggestion Box" by offering financial rewards to staff members who came up with ideas that either:

1. Saved the company money or
2. Helped the company grow.

The business owners were amazed at some of the ideas that the people "doing the job" came up with. They were able to reduce inventory costs by nearly 30 percent while still offering quality products. And, several of the ideas for spinoff products were well received by the company's clients thus generating greater income.

$$$

When you create your meeting agendas, include who you believe needs to be a party to each topic of discussion. Give them advance notice of this so they can prepare. It can be embarrassing for a meeting attendee to have the organizer say, *"Rachel, give us your thoughts on this topic,"* when Rachel didn't know about the topic until she arrived at the meeting and was handed her agenda. Don't risk blind-siding your staff members. You'll waste a lot of time and end up tabling topics or having follow up meetings if attendees are not asked to prepare in advance.

With every meeting, designate someone to take and distribute those notes, including action items, to everyone involved. Choose this person carefully; not everyone takes good notes. Having a designated person assigned the task of ensuring everyone is working from the same list of to-do's—with due dates—will make your meetings ten times more constructive.

Meetings can be extremely productive tools when handled properly. When you show respect for your employees' time, they'll respond in kind—by making the most of the time they spend on their jobs.

Teach by Example

How well you communicate with others rubs off on your team. Your communication style will be an example of how well you expect your team members to communicate amongst themselves. Communicate well with them and you help them learn effective communication skills. You may think that people in business should already have strong communication skills. Unfortunately,

"How to Communicate Effectively with Others 101" is not a course curriculum found in many schools. It can be taught in increments, though, during meetings.

Let's say you used an open question to get someone to elaborate on a point. Thank them for their contribution. Then, explain to the rest of the attendees the strategy used. Suggest that they implement that question type during their interactions for the next few days to get comfortable with what it is and the type of results it brings about.

————————————— **$$$** —————————————

An open question is a question that requires thought on the part of the person asked. These questions yield more information and encourage continued discussion. Most often they start with Who, What, When, Where, Why, or How.

————————————— **$$$** —————————————

Consider building a company library of materials your team members can borrow to enhance their skills. It's best if these are resources you rely on yourself. Encouraging your staff to continue growing right along with the company will enhance the stability of the business overall.

When people are invested in your business, they want to see it do well. When you hire right, you'll have a whole team of people who build your brand, represent you well, and are ready to go for the goal when you need them to take on extra work, train a new hire, or research ways to do their jobs better.

Clearly Communicating Job Responsibilities

As your business grows and you add more people to the team, it's vital that you have clear definitions of each role. When people understand their roles and the expectations of that role, they'll work harder to meet those expectations.

Let's say that you receive a lot of phone calls and decide to hire a receptionist. The role of receptionist may seem simple—answer the phone and direct calls. But, there's way more to it than that. That receptionist may also become the first point of contact between the best lead you've ever gotten for your business—and success. When you think about the value of the first impression of your company, you'll understand what we mean.

Here's what a typical receptionist might say when answering the phone: *"ABC Company."* Or *"ABC Company, who do you need to speak with, please?"* That receptionist would probably get the basic job done. The question is: What happens when the caller doesn't know who they need to speak with? Now, you'll add to the duties of the receptionist to not only know the names of the other people on the team, but to understand their job titles and descriptions well enough to direct calls correctly.

It's all part of building a team that can communicate effectively—and in your favor. Pay attention to how your calls are answered when you contact another place of business. What are they doing or saying that you can learn from? What are the mistakes you should avoid?

Here's how we've taught people to answer calls: *"Thank you for calling ABC Company. How may I direct your call?"* That's a simple, open question that gets the caller to explain why they're calling which will allow the receptionist to determine who the best person is to take the call. Simple? Yes. Effective communication? Yes, again.

It's the little things that make the difference between an average business and a great one. We're sure you've heard the saying, *"Don't sweat the little things."* In business, you DO want to sweat the little things because they all contribute to the overall experience buyers have with your business. And, when buyers have a positive experience, they tell all their friends about it.

Okay, let's add a bit more responsibility to your receptionist. Let's say the caller is interested in one of your products, but the person with the most knowledge about it is out to lunch. Now, the receptionist's duty has become one of capturing that lead—all while giving a positive impression of your company. The receptionist should be able to tell just enough about the product to build the caller's curiosity, but not as much as the salesperson would provide. In exchange, the receptionist will need to be good enough to capture the name and contact information of the caller. Exchange of information is always a two-way street. Don't expect callers to leave their contact information without giving them something in exchange—even if it's a projected time of a return call.

Now, if you were initially thinking that hiring a receptionist was a simple task, do you still feel the same way? Perhaps you thought, *"Anyone can handle that job."* Not if you want the job done well.

It's a similar story with each position you fill in the company. Basically, you want to hire someone with skills and a good attitude. But don't stop there. The more detail about the job responsibilities and expectations you can provide, the more likely it is you'll hire well.

Include cross training in your plan for every new hire. At some point the receptionist will be out of the office, in a meeting or otherwise engaged and someone else will need to fill that position. That person should have the same instructions the receptionist has about how you want the company represented during calls. Consistency is vital to success! This same strategy applies to every position in the company. The more cross training you do, the more effectively your clients will be served and the more efficiently it will run.

Communication Strategies for Counseling a Challenging Employee

It's inevitable that a staff member or employee will create challenges. Not everyone "plays well with others." And, most people embellish their experience and skills on their resumes. That's why it's so important to perform due diligence when hiring.

When you have your duties for each position clearly outlined, counseling someone who's not holding up their end of the bargain is easier. The two most common types of counseling with be with:

1. A relatively new hire who needs to be encouraged and reminded of their job requirements.
2. A more veteran employee who may need a course correction in their attitude or how they treat others.

Let's talk about the newer hire first. Upon hiring, you or your office manager, went over the job responsibilities in detail. The new person was onboarded successfully and seemed to be getting along with the rest of the team. However, his production isn't quite at the level you need and it's time for a one-on-one meeting. It might go like this:

"Hi, Eddie. How are you doing?"

"I'm doing okay. How are you?"

"I'm great, Eddie. Thanks for asking. One of my goals for the business is to grow it steadily and keep up with the needs that growth requires. You were hired because we have a need for your particular skills and talents. I want to check in with you to see how you think you're doing with the responsibilities of your job. What do you like most about it so far?"

Listen carefully.

"I'm glad to hear that. What would you say is the most challenging aspect of your position?"

The reason you ask the question that way is not to put Eddie on the defensive. You want to learn if there's something preventing him from doing his job to your expectations. Perhaps he's not getting clear direction from his immediate supervisor. (Shame on you, if it's you!) Maybe the expectations are beyond his abilities. Maybe he's just not as good as you thought when he was hired. Learn to recognize the difference between excuses and valid reasons when an employee shares any challenges with their job or the job expectations.

If Eddie is only *pretty good* at the job, consider having him take a course relevant to the job requirements to enhance his skills. If he's only performing at an *okay* level and you think he could do more, counsel him starting with the detailed job outline he received upon hiring. Let him know he's not yet on target to meet the expectations of the job. Ask what he thinks needs to be done to improve his level of work. Then, get very specific on each task he's expected to complete. Work together to set new expectations and goals for each task. Then, check in with him in a few days to see how the new plan is working. Most people will perform to the level of expectation you set for them. They like to know they're being acknowledged and offered opportunities to grow.

You need to see improvement within a week of your counseling session. It's up to you how many chances to give someone. If you're seeing progress, you'll probably want to keep them on the team and continue to work with them. If you're not seeing progress, it'll be time for a different type of counseling session.

NOTE: Document the details of your counseling sessions. You will want to have proof that Eddie was terminated "for cause," if it comes to that.

Now, how do you effectively counsel someone who is causing challenges with the other team members? Let's say Charlene has been with your business a while. She's been a strong asset to the company but lately fingers of discontent have been pointed at her by the rest of the team. Maybe she feels threatened by the other folks who've come on board. Maybe she feels she should be in charge of everyone—like a mother hen—because of her seniority.

When you meet one-on-one with Charlene, it might sound like this:

"Hi Charlene. How's it going?"

"Fine. What's up?"

NOTE: Charlene is likely to be on the defensive if she knows other people aren't getting along with her.

"I'd just like to check in to see how things are going with your job responsibilities. I think you're keeping up okay. Are you having any challenges?"

Listen. She'll likely bring up someone else—directing your attention away from her.

"Thanks for sharing that with me. I appreciate your value to the company in doing your job well. As you know, your duties include: (list them). I need you to be careful about stepping outside of those duties. As you know, I have an overall plan for the business and have outlined everyone's job duties as clearly as possible. Unless you're having a specific challenge with someone whose work directly impacts your ability to perform your duties, I'd appreciate if you'd allow me to be the one offering advice to others. We're building a nice team of people here and situations that go outside of each person's job responsibilities tend to rock the boat and waste time. At the level we're all working,

wasting time can negatively impact the bottom line. And, I don't believe either of us wants that to happen."

Charlene is likely to get the point that she's been put on notice with that last statement. However, since we've advised to be clear and concise with all communications, you will want to ask: *"Do you understand what I'm saying?"* If she says anything other than "yes," you will need to be even more direct.

"Charlene, it pains me to do this, but I'm putting you on notice that if you continue to step outside of your job duties, I will have reason to terminate your employment. I have valued your contribution to the team thus far, but as we grow—adding more and more people to the team—I need everyone to work within their job descriptions. Do you understand what I'm saying?"

We covered the two extremes here in our examples. You'll have team members who fall on a wide scale between the two. Some will just need a little nudge to work more effectively. Others will need something closer to the "stern talking to" of a Charlene. The important thing to remember is that everyone is different. When you treat them as individuals, they'll perform better—and that's what you really want, isn't it?

Effective Terminations

There will come a time when you need to terminate someone's employment. Even though people hate to hear the old tried and true *"it's a business decision—nothing personal,"* it will be personal to the person being let go. They will get emotional. They will attempt to cause you to have second thoughts and even guilt about your decision. As with anything important, it's imperative that you preplan and practice what you'll do and say. Here are a few bits of advice when firing someone becomes necessary:

1. If you've done everything you agreed to when the person was hired, providing them with clear goals, job descriptions, the equipment required for the job, and counseling, there will be no guilt. You did your part. They didn't do theirs.

2. Once the decision is made, set a date and time for giving them notice. Do it as soon as possible.

3. Have their final paycheck ready so they can leave the building as soon as notice is given. NOTE: If you're working with remote employees, hopefully you've had a policy of having all their work for you stored on a company-controlled server.

4. Tell no one except your accounting or HR person who will have their final paycheck ready and handle any changes regarding email or software access.

5. Be prepared to re-distribute their work load among other team members until you hire someone new. (This is where your cross-training becomes extremely valuable.)

6. Remain standing. When you invite people to sit down, they're more likely to want to open a whole conversation around the reasons for being let go.

7. Stay calm. Expect the other parties to get emotional, but don't let it get to you.

8. Accept some of the blame for their lack of success with your company. If their level of work doesn't meet your expectations, perhaps you didn't hire right in the first place. Or perhaps they didn't have the potential to grow along with the company as you had expected.

Having effective communication skills will positively impact every aspect of your business. Becoming a good communicator involves presence of mind—truly thinking about what you're going to say. It takes some practice, but with practice, you'll reap the rewards of having done so.

SUMMARY

Being conscious of your communication skills is vital to the success of your startup from the moment you decide to build a team of people to support it. It's important to value the time of your staff members as much as you value your own. Be clear, and direct in your communication about expectations. Learn to use open questions to get your team members to contribute well to the whole.

CHAPTER 7

The Sales Process

Salesmanship is limitless. Our very living is selling.
We are all salespeople.

– JC PENNEY

To repeat our mantra for this entire book, the sales process begins the moment two people interact. It doesn't matter how the connection is made. Every contact with another person is a sales opportunity. Even when connecting with suppliers, your staff members are selling your brand, your company reputation, and information about your products and services.

It doesn't matter if the connection is in person, via phone, video conference, email, or snail mail, every communication for or related to the business is, in essence, selling something and should be treated as such. Please be aware that we don't mean to annoy others with an attitude of sell, sell, sell! Rather, we're referring to the opportunity in every communication to project or reinforce the image of the company in the minds of the people on the receiving end of those communications that they find benefit in working with us.

Inbound Calls

Let's begin with connections over the telephone. Our personal preference is to be, well, personal with the people who contact your business. In other words, if possible, have someone answer the phone rather than using an automated system. While we understand how an automated system enhances the efficiency of your organization, why should the caller (aka potential client) have to do the work of figuring out who they need to speak with?

Recorded messages such as this: *"To access a company directory, press 8. You've reached the ABC company directory, for sales press 1, for accounts payable..."* do little more than frustrate the people who call your company. Why risk having your staff members begin calls with frustrated people on the other end? Your image will be much stronger with everyone when you demonstrate an attitude of service by helping callers every step of the way to doing business with you.

The rule of thumb on the internet is the fewer the clicks, the more likely the sale. The same applies to telephone connections. The faster your caller can connect with the right person, the more likely you are to make the sale, get the response you need from a supplier, or enhance your brand. If you are at a point in your business where you have the luxury of dedicating someone to the task of answering calls, great. If not, every team member should be trained to properly handle incoming calls—no matter the type.

It's important to have a consistent manner, throughout the company, for addressing callers. This training would include the proper words to use when answering calls, and the attitude to put forth. Most people want to do business with a company whose people are uplifting and helpful. When a call comes in, whoever is responsible to answer it should turn away from whatever else they are working on, put a smile on his or her face, and give the caller their full attention.

Believe it or not, a smile can be "heard" over the telephone. Think about it, if you made a call to a business and the person on the other end sounded as if you just interrupted them or that they're distracted, how important would you feel? Not very, right? Your number one goal in selling is to do the things necessary to help people to like you, trust you, and want to listen to you. When you make others feel important that goal is more easily achieved.

If you do rely on an automated system to answer your incoming calls, do your best to keep the options limited to a very few. Have the person on your team with the best speaking voice record the prompts. Or, have them done professionally. You might even want to mix up the recordings by alternating male and female voices. Keep your messages light and even a little bit fun. Being different (in a good way) makes you memorable.

Whether live or recorded, be certain to thank callers for reaching out to your business in your initial greeting. In the case of having your people answer the calls, have them identify themselves with both first and last names. Have them ask the callers, *"How may I help you?"* Or, *"How may I assist you?"* Or, *"How may I direct your call?"*

A "how" question is an open-ended question that requires the caller to explain why they called or what information they're seeking. This allows your staff person to direct them to the proper person in your business more quickly than if you had them ask no question at all. The person asking the questions controls the conversation. By not asking a question, the caller is in control of the conversation and the person who answered the call may end up listening to the caller's life story.

Ask callers for their first and last names, and for their contact information as soon as possible. The purpose of this is to be able to reach back out to them should *Murphy's Law* intervene and disconnect the call. Then, give the caller the name of the best person to answer their questions or to provide the information they require before transferring the call. If that person has a direct line, also provide that number to the caller—only if it's company policy to do so. If the use of direct lines is restricted, at least provide the caller with an extension number in case they need to call after hours in the future.

In-House Voice Mail

The outgoing voice mail messages of each staff member should be consistent. Use something like the message below as the beginning of a pattern for your employees:

"This is _____. Thank you for calling. I apologize for not being available. Please leave me a detailed message including the most convenient time for me to reach you. I'll be happy to return your call."

For your sales team, you might have them add to the end of that message *"...and serving your* (type of service you provide) *needs."*

Outbound Calls

Outbound calls should be well thought through before being made. Remember, every contact is a sales presentation. It should be treated as such. That means some preparation is required. We are not saying to invest hours of time into preparing for all outbound calls. That would end up being a business-killer. For sales-specific calls, yes, they require more planning and preparation. However, even a quick call to let a client know about a delivery date, or to resolve a customer service issue deserves some thought before picking up the phone.

Treat each contact as you would a face-to-face meeting with a client. Consider training your team members to jot down a quick agenda for each phone call. It may look something like this:

- Greet & thank
- Establish rapport
- Explain the reason for the call
- Deliver the message/Ask for information
- Share additional info
- Make a commitment to the next contact
- Thank and end call

This simple process only takes a minute and it may only take three or four minutes to deliver, but it helps the callers on your team to clear their minds and focus on the reason for the call as well as the result they're anticipating. It also helps to eliminate those *"Oh, I forgot to tell her about..."* moments. Such moments can lead to an embarrassing second call that lowers the other person's conviction about your team member's competence. And thus, the competence of your company as a whole. Why risk it? Teach everyone the quick and simple strategy of jotting down an agenda for each outbound call.

Leaving Voice Mail Messages

It may also be helpful to develop a pattern for leaving messages when your staff members make outbound calls. Isn't it frustrating when people leave you messages in which they haven't spoken clearly, or they left their number so quickly that you have to listen to the message more than once to get it, so you can return their call? Make a concerted effort never to do that to anyone you call.

Here's the pattern for leaving voice mail messages:

- Greeting
- Identify yourself
- State the reason for your call
- Leave your phone number and best time you can be reached
- Repeat your phone number
- *"I look forward to speaking with you."*

For a sales call, the "reason for your call" part of the call really needs some planning. Help your sales team to set a goal of never being unprepared when they have to leave a voice message. Start by always assuming the person being called will be unavailable. Even when there's a scheduled time to speak with a client or potential client, stuff happens. So, preparation is the key to success.

Messages for calls to existing clients would be relevant to their product or service—a delivery or a customer service issue. These messages should be delivered in a pleasant manner and with an attitude of servitude.

A sales call to a *potential* client requires a different message. The goal here is to build enough curiosity about the benefits of your product (not the features), that they want to call you back or that they accept your next call (in case they're using voice mail as a call screening device).

An example of this would be: *"Hello, Mr. Smith. This is Bob Jones calling with some ideas to save your company money while increasing employee job satisfaction. Explaining how this works will take less than seven minutes of your time. I can be reached at 800-555-1234 between 2 and 5 this afternoon. I'll repeat my number for you. It's 800-555-1234. I look forward to helping your company save money. If I don't hear back from you today, I'll reach out to you again tomorrow morning. I sincerely hope you're having a spectacular day!"*

Failure to plan the best way to handle the telephone in the best interest of your company and your clients is a plan for failure. Get everyone on your team involved in the process to come up with your ideal plan. It shouldn't be a major undertaking. With everyone's contributions, you'll get more of a 'buy in' for them to use it. Then, inspire everyone to use it properly. The pattern of consistency across your organization in how you handle both in and outbound calls will make a difference in everyone's perception of your business.

Email Messages

It's important to establish a pattern for email messages as well. For starters, everyone in the company should use the same style for their signature lines. Take a few moments to analyze the signatures of those who send you messages. Find a pattern you like and can see the benefit of. Then develop your custom signature pattern and have everyone in the company use it for consistency in branding.

Nothing puts a dent in credibility faster than emails that are dashed off quickly without review. Spelling errors demonstrate carelessness. Misrepresentation of companies destroys more sales than anything else. And the sad aspect of those occurrences is that they can be avoided. Teach your team members the value of re-reading all messages before hitting the "Send" button. The minute or two it takes to check the wording used in those messages can literally save your company's life.

It's important to realize that an email communication is more like a letter than an in-person conversation. The recipient cannot "hear" the tone of voice in which the words are meant to be delivered. So, it's critical that the wording in emails be considered very carefully. These messages need to be kept simple and be extremely clear. If you doubt whether or not a written message is clear enough, consult with another staff member or schedule a phone or in-person meeting to ensure the proper message is delivered.

Online Video Meetings

When using a service for an online video meeting, always get on the call a few minutes prior to the appointed time. Don't risk finding out last minute that your internet service is sketchy or even down completely, or that there's an upgrade in the service that requires a computer reboot. Also, don't risk the other party or parties being on the call first and watching you scramble as you settle into your seat to join them.

Give yourself a once-over in your video camera to ensure the lighting on your face (or on whatever you're demonstrating) is good. Poor lighting = poor delivery. Also, look to see what else is in the video frame. Is there a plant in the background that looks like it's either not well-cared-for or sticking up out of your head? What else do you see in the frame? A messy desk? Your jacket, purse, or cell phone? Any posters or comics that might not be appropriate for a client to see (even though you and the in-house team love them)? Be like a director and see that the stage is set for the visual image of the meeting to deliver the message you want.

In-Person Meetings

In sales, there are four keys to giving successful presentations:

1. Prepare
2. Practice
3. Perform
4. Perfect.

Each step builds on the one before it. If you don't prepare properly, you'll practice the wrong strategy; your performance will fall short of the mark; and you simply won't be able to perfect your presentation.

When planning for an in-person meeting, you'll not only research the potential client's company and key representatives, but their location. Nothing makes you look worse than to be late to your meeting because you were unaware of the fact there's only one entrance into their office complex neighborhood and it's partially blocked by construction which means you can only get into the parking lot if you're coming from the West. With the help of technology, you can receive up-to-the-minute details on your route including if an accident occurs that causes a detour. Take advantage of that technology, but also plan an alternate route just in case.

As part of your preparation, consider what you'll wear to the presentation and what materials you will take with you. The rule of thumb for attire is to dress like a person your potential client would turn to for advice. If you're working with the manager of a mom and pop restaurant, you might dress a little more casually than if you're working with the manager of a corporate HR department. Learn how they dress while on the job and dress similarly or just a little more professionally. The last thing you want is to have what you're wearing distract from your presentation or begin the presentation with potential clients feeling uncomfortable.

While it's easy to decide to take everything, you might possibly need with you to your meetings, the impression you make when you arrive with a giant presentation kit might not be the best. A better thought would be to take everything you might possibly need *for this client*. In other words, do your homework on the client's current situation and needs. Prepare for that. The more customization you can do, the better. You won't waste anyone's time and you'll be speaking directly to their specific needs. That will go a long way toward achieving the goal of a closed sale.

Once you feel you have the information you need to create a powerful, engaging presentation, start practicing. Deliver the presentation in your head. Fine-tune how you'll move, when you'll direct the potential client's attention by pointing out a feature or key information. Then, perform it aloud.

If you'll be delivering your presentation standing in front of a group, by all means, stand when you practice and perform. Deliver your presentation to an associate or loved one. If no one is available at the time you're doing this, consider using a full-length mirror. Pay attention to how you move. Body language often speaks more loudly than words.

Once you feel you have the details of your presentation fine-tuned, work on perfecting your delivery. When you deliver your entire presentation several times before the actual presentation, you'll display more confidence when in front of others, which equates to competence in the minds of your buyers.

Achieve Success in Your Mind First

The comic motion picture *Major League* is about a baseball team on its last legs rising to take the World Series. It's a slapstick-funny movie, but there is an interesting small bit in one scene that illustrates an important lesson for anyone in a start-up position. Just before the big game one of the players sits off to himself, closes his eyes, and begins to make slight waving gestures with his hand, clearly lost in thought. He's playing the upcoming game in his head. He's visualizing all the things that could happen in the game and how he should react to them. Later, when he runs out onto the field he's halfway to victory because he's already won in his mind. The lesson should be obvious. Success is accomplished only when it is mind accomplished.

The great Chinese general and military strategist, Sun Tzu said, *"Every battle is won before it is ever fought."* You've probably heard that several times, but have you ever stopped to consider what that really means? Of all the elements that comprise success in business, preparation is perhaps the most important. It's the foundation that supports the entire structure or sets up its collapse and failure.

How Does a Start-up Entrepreneur Get Prepared?

First, eliminate all unnecessary activities. Even though this is an obvious point, it can be much harder than it seems. For example, a professional ghost writer we know related that many of his, as he says, "so-called authors" never get around to actually writing their business books, great American novels, screenplays or angry letters to the editor because they're consumed with *preparing* to write. Studying writing books, taking writing courses, conducting research, working with editors and suppliers is important, *but it's not writing.*

We've met countless businesspeople who are trapped by the same kind of misguided thinking. They're so busy getting ready to conduct business that they never get around to conducting business.

What we're saying isn't contradictory. Preplanning and preparation are essential to success, but preparation must be focused like a laser on the specific areas necessary to assure success. Many of the activities you will need to eliminate are attractive. They appear to be important. Others might tell you they're necessary. The start-up professional must ask, *"Is this* really *necessary?"* And he must ask it time and time again throughout the process of founding and managing a successful business. If the activity won't get you where you want to be – effectively and efficiently, eliminate it. Or at least relegate it to the back burner where it belongs.

Time for Organization

"Work smarter not harder" is a time-worn adage. But do you know why it's time worn? Because it's the truth. It's an undeniable fact that has been proven over time. Effective time planning is one of the most productive methods for working smarter.

One of the great things about time planning is that it doesn't take a lot of time to do. If you'll just invest a mere ten minutes a day in planning, you will be amazed at how much you can accomplish in that day. This simple task requires a shift in thinking for most start-up professionals. You may have heard and have even been taught that planning is an excruciating, time-consuming, must-do challenge. We agree with the "must do," but take exception to the rest of that belief.

Take that ten minutes and write down the six most important things you must do that day (or the following one). Estimate how much time to allocate to each task and assign the appropriate timeframes to get them done. If the task is a big one, break it down into smaller and more manageable bits and assign the necessary time to accomplish those bits. Build in gaps between tasks to allow for things that run over your projected time frames. Otherwise, you'll set up a negative reaction of running late on tasks all day.

Many well-known successful entrepreneurs operate by including short breaks in their days. Those short breaks allow them to stretch their legs, catch a breath of fresh air, or otherwise reinforce their energy for each task.

Get into Character

One particularly effective way many actors take on a role is by the outward-inward approach. That means they get into character by taking on the outward appearance of that character with costumes, make up, hair styles and so on. The inner man is created by the outward appearance. You can do the same thing. Regardless of how you feel in the morning, tell yourself with conviction that you're going to have a great day. Think it. Look in the mirror and say it. Sing it in the shower. Remember, every day you have the opportunity to play the role of a lifetime. Make it an Oscar worthy performance.

The Most Important Sale You Will Ever Make

The most important sale for most people is often the hardest sale to make. That sale is selling your abilities to yourself!

You are the key to your own success and that of your start-up business. If you don't believe in yourself, no one else will either. They won't want to follow your lead. When it comes to believing in yourself, it's not a matter of believing that you *can* do this. It's a matter of you *must* do this. A start-up entrepreneur must have an incredible drive to succeed. Otherwise he or she would never begin.

Believe in yourself. Raise your energy level to high-performance standards. If you're going to influence and motivate your staff, your prospects and your customers, you have to be fully in character all the time. Make getting into character a part of your routine. Make the coming day's success mind-accomplished. Visualize it. Touch, taste, hear, and smell that success. Surround yourself with a mental shield that will never permit the slightest bit of negative thinking to influence your performance.

And then get to work!

The Seven Steps to the Sales Process

Selling isn't something that happens by itself. Unless you're in retail and offering low ticket products such as ice cream or candy, few people will connect with you and simply say, *"I want to buy this."* On the other side of the equation, few people you hire will have a solid enough understanding of the sales process to just start selling for you with little or no help. They need training.

Until you reach a point where you can hire a sales manager or in-house trainer, the responsibility for training will fall to you—or at least it'll be your call on using any outside services for training.

There are thousands of nuances that make up the art and science of selling. No one book could possibly cover them all. However, we'll do our best in the rest of this chapter to get you started on the path to sales success.

The seven steps of the sales process include:

1. Prospecting – where and how to find new potential clients
2. Initial Contact – making direct contact with those potential clients
3. Qualification – determining whether your potential clients have the need, interest and ability to become satisfied clients
4. Presentation or Demonstration – employing strategies to help your potential clients envision themselves owning the benefits of your product
5. Addressing Concerns – helping people overcome the natural fears that arise when making buying decisions
6. Closing Sales – using effective strategies to clearly and directly ask for the business and get a commitment
7. Getting Referrals – how to get your clients to refer you to others

Prospecting

Where are your clients going to come from? There's an old saying, *"Build a better mousetrap and the world will beat a path to your door."* Sounds wonderful, doesn't it? The only way you'll get the world to beat a path to your door is to build the path, and then tell the world where it is—not just what it leads to.

As a solo entrepreneur or small business owner, you'll want to quickly learn strategies to generate leads for business. One of the simplest strategies is called the *Three-Foot Rule*. How it works is that you speak with anyone who comes within three feet of you to determine one of two things:

1. Are they a potential candidate for your product?

2. Do they know someone who is a potential candidate for your product?

Some people will fit both scenarios. They will be interested in your product and know others who would be interested.

You and anyone who works with you will inevitably be involved in either social or business networking situations where you have the opportunity to get to know others and share what you do. In these situations, it's helpful to have a few conversation-starter questions ready. These would be those open questions covered earlier. Remember? Open questions typically begin with Who, What, When, Where, Why, and How. They require thought on the part of the hearer and don't lend themselves to one-word replies.

Here are a few examples:

"How do you know the hosts?"

"Where do you live?"

"What type of business are you involved in?"

Develop other questions, the answers to which tell you if each person you speak with might be a good candidate for your product or service.

During these networking opportunities, always ask the new people you meet to introduce you to others they know at the event. Beginning with an introduction often makes starting a conversation much easier.

Initial Contact

When you first make contact, you have one goal: To help people like you, trust you, and want to listen to you. Once you accomplish that, the next few steps become a lot easier.

To help people to like and trust you, make them feel important. They are important, aren't they? Of course. Everyone is. Be warm and friendly but remain professional. When meeting people in person or via video chat, begin your contact with a smile and eye contact. The eye contact aspect can be tricky via video chat, but with a little practice, you'll manage.

When contacting someone via the telephone, always smile. As mentioned before, a smile can be heard over the telephone.

If your initial contact is via email, text, or any other form of print, begin with a warm greeting. Don't just jump right into your message. You wouldn't do that if you met them in person. Don't do it in any other form of contact either.

Express gratitude. An abundance of gratitude generates abundance in return. You're asking people to give you their time and attention. Always be grateful for that. They could certainly be doing something else with their time, couldn't they?

Use their names. Getting names right is critical to your success in sales—even if the "sale" is building a friendship or relationship with a co-worker.

Come close to matching the speed and volume of speech used by the other person. If they speak slowly, it's not necessary to slow down to their same speed. Just be aware of whether they speak faster or slower than your normal rate of speech and be ready to adjust your speed a bit.

- If you speak too quickly for them, they won't follow what you're saying, and they'll likely get confused. And, a confused mind says, "*no.*"
- If you speak too slowly, they may wonder if you're doing so because you're not the brightest bulb in the pack which will dent your credibility with them.

People like to buy from people who are like them. Try to be "like them" in the speed with which you speak. Beware, however, of changing your normal speech pattern too much or too quickly. Doing so is likely to derail your train of thought.

Search for common ground. When you're truly interested in other people, this is easy. Your common ground could, literally, be the ground you're standing on if you met in a park or at an event such as a concert or play. If you both have children playing sports or around the same age, that's common ground. If you both have the same challenge your product resolves, that's the best!

Give a sincere compliment. When you pay attention to details, you can always find something to compliment another person on, such as: their style of clothing, a piece of jewelry, their position in the company, or their friendly demeanor.

During your initial contact with people, you also want to build their curiosity about you and your product. Interest is created by your attitude, belief, and conviction about the benefits of your product.

Qualification

The qualification step in the sales process is where you start asking specific questions about the interest your buyer has shown during your initial contact. Do not ask questions as if you're ticking them off a list or grilling them like the police do in the movies. Keep it conversational but use the following questions in your conversation to get the information you need. Your goal with their answers is to determine if they're truly qualified to own your product or service.

1. *What do you have now? What are you using now? How are you handling that challenge now?*
2. *What do you like (or enjoy) about what you're doing now?*
3. *In considering a new solution for this challenge, what would you like to see? What would you like to alter or change about what you're doing now?*
4. *If we're fortunate to have a solution that meets your needs, is there someone else you would want to consult with about making a change? Who, other than yourself, would be involved in making a final decision? What is the normal process your company goes through in acquiring new products and services?*

Here's what you're likely to hear in response to these questions:

1. *"I'm not doing anything to fix this now."* Or, *"I'm using* (a competitor's product).*"* If they're not trying to resolve the challenge either they haven't found a solution they feel confident about or they don't feel it's a big enough challenge to address. If it's the latter, this person might not be qualified to own your product. If you can't build a case for ownership, you may want to switch gears, asking who else they know with a similar challenge and go for a referred lead instead of a sale.

2. *"I like the fact that it does...."* People rarely speak about features of products. They'll tell you about the benefits they like. When you move into your presentation, remember to mention the features they tell you about.

3. *"I really like X, but it would be great if it did Y."* Once again, your buyer will likely talk about benefits. If they really enjoy something about their existing product, it will be important for them to have that benefit in something new. If your product has it, great! If it doesn't, hopefully the other benefits of your product will outweigh what's missing enough that the buyer will be willing to try your product.

4. *"No one. I would make the decision on my own."* Or, *"I need to consult with the department that will be using the product."* Or, *"I need to get approval on a purchase order from my manager."* If the buyer you're speaking with is the sole decision-maker, great! If they need to consult with someone else, you may want to deliver just enough product information to inspire the buyer to arrange for any other decision-maker to be involved in your full-blown presentation. This may postpone your presentation

to another date, but that's better than giving a presentation to someone who can't make a purchasing decision today.

The answers to those four simple questions will give you enough information to decide whether your "buyer" is truly qualified to own your product because they:

1. Have a need,
2. Your product matches their need, and
3. They could make a buying decision.

Presentation or Demonstration

This is the step in the sales process that most salespeople enjoy. They like orchestrating demonstrations of the incredible product you've created. Sadly, most salespeople memorize one single script for demonstrating the product and feel they have to deliver every detail of it. They fail to be flexible enough to deliver the presentation within the parameter of needs of each potential client. It takes time and practice to get to this point, but those who do will be your best salespeople.

The purpose of the presentation is to create conviction in the mind of the buyer—conviction that your product solves a need they have. It's really that simple. How do you create conviction? You do it based on the information gained during the qualification step of the sales process. There you learned what the buyer likes and dislikes about their current situation, right? Now, you present your product in light of that information.

We suggest you review the features of your product, but in such a way as to cover what each feature means to the buyer.

That's their benefit of owning it. When the benefits you present match the needs they've expressed, in their minds this becomes evidence that your product just may be the solution they're seeking. In essence, the features/benefits aspect of presenting draws an outline of the solution. Then, the salesperson's job is to fill in the rest of that picture to such a degree that the end result is a closed sale. It becomes a no-brainer, if you will, for the buyer to say *"yes"* to your offering.

Be cautious when speaking about your product to avoid saying things like, *"I love the color."* Or, *"This is what I like best."* Your potential clients probably won't care what you like. You're trying to sell them something. Instead, mention *what others have liked* about your product or a creative use someone else came up with for it.

What you *can* do regarding your feelings about your product is to tell your story about how you became involved with it. You can also tell of your personal experiences with the product—as long as you've really used and benefited from it. Add to your story the testimonials of other satisfied clients. This will all build confidence in your buyers that your product is and does what you say.

Most people buy to either avoid or eliminate a pain they're feeling, or to gain some type of pleasure. It's the *Pain/Pleasure Principle.* Keep that principle in the back of your mind when speaking about your product. Which is it for this particular client? Are they wanting to eliminate a pain or gain pleasure? This is an important nuance of selling. Knowing the answer will help you direct what you say to their specific desires… and close more sales.

Addressing Concerns

The sooner you face the fact that people are going to have objections or raise concerns about your product or your service, the better. It's a normal part of the selling process. It actually means they're interested. They're interested enough to feel pulled toward owning it. And the natural reaction to that *"pull"* is to pull back.

Most people don't want to be considered an easy sale. So, when they're feeling pulled toward handing over their credit cards or writing checks, they tend to pause. The most common type of pause used is to raise an objection. The objection, or concern as we call it, requires the salesperson to address it. It allows the buyer to sit back and catch his or her breath before making a final decision.

What causes this to happen?

Sometimes buyers simply feel things are moving too quickly. They're feeling compelled to part with their hard-earned money and want to give the decision a second (or third) thought.

Buyers may have unanswered questions. As they feel the urge to move forward, they think of something that wasn't covered or perhaps it was and they're now not 100% certain they understood it correctly.

What matters when you hear an objection or concern is that you know the buyer is leaning toward making a purchase. The hardest sale to make is one where a buyer listens to everything you have to say and then does nothing. You don't know where to go with the sales process or even if there's still a process going on.

When you hear stalls, objections or concerns, be happy. You're still in the game and the buyer has shown interest. It's now your job to get them off the fence on the side of ownership.

The Most Common Concerns

The most common concerns are usually money issues. You'll often hear things like this:

- It costs too much.
- It just isn't in the budget right now.
- I think I can get this cheaper.

When you hear these types of stalls, it's your job to create some urgency or to otherwise rationalize making the decision now. Buyers use money stalls because they work to their advantage. Average salespeople will hear them and start lowering the price of their product. Some will even lower it so much that they hardly make anything on the sale. Don't be like that!

If you want to give product away just do it and write it off as goodwill for your company. Don't negotiate the amount you're willing to accept for your product unless you're prepared to do the same for every friend, relative or associate this person sends your way.

We'll cover a few examples of this to give you an idea of how to handle money stalls.

1. It costs too much.

You'll hear this one a lot. It's probably the single most common stall in sales of every kind of product. Let's say your product is $100. When you hear this, don't start thinking about the $100.

Ask, *"How much 'too much' do you feel it is?"* The idea is to get to the amount they think is too much. You have to know a dollar amount to work with. It's doubtful people would say $100 because they expect to pay *something* for your product, right?

Once you know how much *"too much"* it is, you work on justifying that amount. If your product is something that will be used every day for at least a year, divide that *"too much"* number by 52 weeks or even 365 days to reduce it to an amount that's not even worth objecting to. *"I understand how you feel, Emma. Understanding that you'll use this air cleaner every day for at least the next year, that $30 you're concerned about is only about 8 cents per day. When you look at it that way, do you think you should keep from experiencing all the benefits of breathing cleaner air?"*

2. I just isn't in the budget.

Know that people who have budgets are typically much smarter about managing their money and seeking bargains. They like being known for those traits. Rather than fighting with them over the money amount, use the budget to help them make the buying decision. You might say something like this:

"I can understand that, Jim. That's why I contacted you in the first place. I'm fully aware of the fact that every well-managed business controls the flow of its money with a carefully planned budget. The budget is a necessary tool for every company to give direction to their goals. However, the tool itself doesn't dictate how the company is run. It must be flexible. You, as the controller of that budget, retain for yourself the right to flex it in the best interest of the company's financial present and competitive future, don't you?

What we have been examining here today is a system, which will allow your company an immediate and continuing competitive edge. Tell me, under these conditions, will your budget flex, or will it dictate your actions?"

With minor adjustments, this can be used in a consumer sale as well. After all we all choose where our money goes by using budgets, right?

3. I think I can get this cheaper.

"That may well be true, John. And, after all, in today's economy, we all want the most for our money. A truth that I have learned over the years is that the cheapest price is not always what we really want. Most people look for three things when making an investment:

1. *the finest quality*
2. *the best service, and*
3. *the lowest price.*

I have never yet found a company that could offer the finest quality and the best service for the lowest price. I'm curious, John, for your long-term happiness, which of the three would you be most willing to give up? The finest quality? Excellent service? Or, low price?"

Re-read those three stalls and the responses we've provided. You'll soon realize that your job is not just demonstrating products. It's helping people to rationalize owning them.

Closing Sales

There's a simple little step between addressing concerns or handling objections and actually asking for the sale. It's called *"test closing."* It's a way to determine if you've really reached the point of the buyer making a decision or if there's something else preventing them from going ahead. With test closing, you don't come across as a pushy or aggressive salesperson.

A test close could be as simple as this question: *"How are you feeling about all of this, Mark?"* With this open question, your buyer is likely to answer with something along the lines of *"pretty good,"* or *"I'm still not certain."* If, instead of testing the waters, you ask directly for his business, you risk changing his level of interest in the entire process. When you get an affirmative response to a test closing question, you know the buyer is ready to go ahead. This little strategy makes for smooth transitions into closing sales. Take advantage of it!

When you believe the buyer is ready to go ahead with owning your product or starting your service, getting the business can be as simple as filling out your order form (paper or online) and asking how the buyer would like to complete the transaction. Credit card? Check? Mention whatever form of payment you accept. Then ask for their signature on the order.

Please note that we said to ask for their *signature*. You may also use the term *authorization* since that's what many of the credit card companies use. Take a bit of advice and do not ask them to *sign* anything. The word *sign* could cancel out all the work you've done up to this point. Many of us have been told by our elders and even contemporaries who've had bad past experiences to *"Never sign anything without reading the fine print."* Right? That word has become a virtual stop sign in the world of sales. It's killed sales that would have gone through. It's started a process of second-guessing decisions. Eliminate it from your vocabulary unless your product is *signage.* Then, only use it when describing your product.

When you and the buyer both agree that there's no sale to be made right now, there's still an opportunity to learn from the interaction. Use what is called the *Lost Sale Close.* It's great for when you have nothing to lose. It goes like this: Pack up your materials. Thank the buyer for their time. Then ask for help and clarification of what you did wrong. We're not saying you're "wrong," but use that term with the buyer. This can be a humbling experience, and it can lead to knowledge that catapults your business to greater success. Say something along the lines of this: *"Pardon me, John, before I leave may I apologize for not doing my job today? You see, if I had not been inept, I would have said the things necessary to convince you of the value of my product. Because I didn't, you and your company/family will not be enjoying the benefits of our product and service and, believe me, I am truly sorry. John, I believe in my product. So I don't make the same mistake again, will you please tell me what I did wrong, and please be very candid with me."*

When buyers like and trust you, they'll be open to answering this question if… you asked it in a warm and sincere manner. Generally, people are helpful when asked for help. Listen to what they have to say. Take notes. Thank them for their input.

Another benefit of this strategy is that often buyers will tell you something that allows you to move back into your presentation and save the sale. Perhaps they bring up something you forgot to cover or a concern they weren't sure how to address. It's happened. Try it. What have you got to lose?

Getting Referred Leads

How do you get referred leads for new business? You ask for them! It really is almost that simple. Asking satisfied clients to provide you with contact information for friends, relatives, and business associates is a natural step in the sales process. Unfortunately, this step is overlooked by a large percentage of businesses and salespeople.

It's helpful to set the stage for asking for referrals early in your presentation. You might say something like this, *"Pamela, our business, like yours, grows by referral. If we are able to help you resolve your* (type of product/service) *challenges and you are 100% satisfied with our service, you wouldn't mind telling others about it, would you?*

You see, as we cover the benefits of our product/service during our time together, someone else you know might come to mind— an associate or relative who might have a similar challenge. If that happens, would you please provide me with their contact information, so I can reach out to them like I did with you? Would that be okay?" Most people will be agreeable at this point because they're under no obligation. They haven't become a satisfied client yet. When they do purchase your product or service, you simply remind them of this request and ask for the contact information for three to five people.

What usually happens when attempting to get referrals is that salespeople ask, *"Do you know anyone else who might be interested in our product?"* The knee-jerk response most people have to this question is the same you hear used when retail people say, *"May I help you?"* The answer is, *"No."*

To avoid that reaction, you ask instead, *"Who, among your co-workers could benefit from this product?"* *"Who, in your exercise class would enjoy learning about this as well?"* You ask clients about specific groups of people they know—groups they've mentioned in conversation. When you ask for three to five names, you'll likely get at least two. And, when people turn to their contacts list in their phones to get you the information, they'll scroll past plenty of other names to consider.

SUMMARY

There are a lot of nuances in the game of selling. Mastering even a few increases your odds of generating sales. After every presentation to sell or get others involved in your business, analyze what you said, how they responded and how you might do things differently the next time. Become a student of selling!

CHAPTER 8

Negotiation Skills

Everything is negotiable.
Whether or not the negotiation is easy is another thing.

– CARRIE FISHER

The art, the science, and the skill of effective negotiating can be summed up in five essential steps.

1. Preparation
2. Information Exchange
3. Concessions
4. Close the Sale
5. Follow up

If the concept of mastering these steps at first appears daunting, consider the fact that: You're already halfway there.

How is that possible, you ask? It's important that you realize and understand this basic fact: you already have within you all that you need to become a successful negotiator. You just have to work a bit to bring those skills to the surface, so you can put them to use.

Look at it the way we see things. You already know how to read, write, count, talk, think and chew gum at the same time. These skills may be underdeveloped for us specific to negotiating—or even dormant—but they're already in place and ready for you to fully master and put them to work. You've just started and already you're far ahead of where you thought you'd be!

Essential Step #1 – Preparation

Effective negotiation demands effective preparation. You would never start out on a business trip without packing your suit, your cell phone, credit cards, computer, and necessary backup documents. The same principle applies to negotiation – be prepared. This is a simple, three-stage process.

Stage One. Have an agenda. Know what you want and need to accomplish and have your goal or goals firmly established in mind. What's your bottom line in the negotiation? Determine that and build your agenda around at least achieving that and, ideally, achieving a lot more.

Stage Two. Know your position. How close are you to achieving your agenda? What roadblocks are in your way? How can you go around, over, under or through them? How much can you afford to give and still come out ahead? What's your actual bail out point? What are your options at each step of the process? Are you dealing with someone who has the authority to say *"yes"* to your proposal? If not, how do you find and connect with this person?

Stage Three. Know the other person's position. You may not like it. You may not even fully understand it, but you must know it. The old line *"walk a mile in another man's shoes"* applies here. Once you know his or her position you can tailor your presentation to show how your product, service or concept ideally matches that position. If the position of the other party is not to your advantage, you can reframe your questions to your advantage and continue to recommend your much better position.

Essential Step #2 – Information Exchange

We live in a time known as *"the information age"* and for good reason. Never in the history of the earth has more information been more readily available to more people than during our lifetime. The amount of information available instantly at your fingertips is astounding when you think about it. Information is an essential tool and the free flow of information is vital to successful negotiations. That flow must go both ways. Each party has a responsibility to send and receive essential information to the other party, so a successful negotiation can be concluded. You keep the information flowing by following a few basic rules.

- Ask pertinent questions.
- Avoid "fluff" questions unless needed just to keep things moving.
- Be an active listener. Never focus on formulating the next question until you understand the answer to the one you just asked.

- Ask open-ended questions that require extended, information-providing responses. For example, *"Is XYZ important?"* can be answered with a conversation-stopping *"yes"* or *"no."* Rephrased to an open-ended, *"Why is XYZ important?"* requires an extended answer that should provide you with valuable insights and information.

Essential Step #3. Prepare Concessions

Compromise is usually an element in negotiations. The *"give a little get a little"* practice comes in to play throughout this type of conversation. Prepare a series of concessions in advance that you would be willing to use. When and if you have to employ concessions, begin with the smallest, least costly, least painful one and then move up the list to those that are more financially challenging *only if you must.* That doesn't mean you should expect to give away the farm just to get what you need from the process.

As with many things in life, perception can become reality. There's no use in offering a concession if the other party doesn't see it as a concession of genuine value. In a situation like that, all you've done is given away something without gaining anything in return. The more valuable the other party perceives your concession, the better – even if the concession, in reality, costs you little or nothing.

Essential Step #4. Close the Sale

Once a negotiation is completed and each party is satisfied an amazing and sometimes unfortunate thing can happen – buyer's remorse. Each party suddenly and inexplicably begins to regret the outcome of the negotiation. Buyer's remorse may take days or weeks to hit, or it can also be instantaneous. It is essential that both parties approve the paperwork, letter of agreement, memo, or cocktail napkin immediately before buyer's remorse can set it. Don't doubt this. Negotiate and then *get the written approval as quickly as possible.*

Essential Step #5. Follow up

Follow up on every negotiation happens in two stages: internal and external.

The internal follow up is an evaluation of how well you performed during the process. It's a self-evaluation done after every negotiation. How well did I do? Where did I make mistakes? How would I handle that situation differently now? What does the other party think of me and the negotiation? Ask a lot of questions of yourself and answer them honestly. Those answers will provide invaluable insights for your in-person follow up and in your next negotiation.

The external follow up is done with the other party in the negotiation. Call, text, email or visit to make sure that the agreement and all terms are being honored and that the agreed-on schedule is being kept.

Your integrity is your greatest asset. Always negotiate with total integrity regardless of what the other people in the organization, business or industry are doing. Some of the toughest, most challenging negotiators we've ever encountered were men and women of the highest integrity. Playing tough doesn't mean playing dirty. Word gets around. People talk. And the ones who act dishonestly may win something now and then, but they miss out on other successes because honest people just don't want to deal with dishonest people. Keep your integrity and your business in good shape.

Create Successful Negotiations by Creating Win/Win Scenarios

We believe in coming out on top in negotiations, but we don't believe, as so many misguided entrepreneurs do, that coming out on top means sending the other party to the bottom. Best results are achieved when a win/win scenario is achieved. For one thing, when both parties are happy they'll want to do more business together. Everybody wins again down the road. On the other hand, a win/lose scenario leaves one party unhappy and possibly aching for some payback later.

Creating a win/win scenario doesn't have to be challenging. It's cost-effective and fast. And it builds long-term business. Here are a few guidelines.

1. <u>Keep a positive attitude</u>. Your mind creates what you tell it to create. Fill your head with realistic images of success before, during, and after the negotiation. Action follows thought, so think proactively and keep those thoughts positive.

2. <u>Be aware</u>. Monitor yourself and the other party for signs that could affect the negotiations, such as fatigue, lack of enthusiasm, indecisiveness, anger, frustration, sudden interest in a specific point, and so on. Awareness can keep you from going down the wrong path or help by pointing out a shortcut to a successful conclusion.

3. <u>Understand the role perception plays in the negotiation</u>. Your strength or even your weakness can be used as an

effective negotiating tool if you are aware of how the other party views the process. You can use your awareness skills to find ways to use perception to your advantage.

4. Be prepared. It's important to have all your documentation available. It's just as important that you know all that you need to know so thoroughly that you can use documentation for back up and not as a rescue device.

5. Keep your integrity. Once lost, a reputation is a very difficult treasure to regain. Think and act for long-term success and not just for a *"killing"* at the moment.

6. Pay attention. Everything affects everything else. Be aware of what is going on around you at all times. When you pick up on clues, subtle or not so subtle, adjust your presentation accordingly and proceed to a successful conclusion.

7. Don't rush. Take enough time to make sure all your bases are covered and that you are fully prepared. Control the speed of the process so you can deliver the positive outcome.

8. Play the "what if" game. Throughout the process offer *"what if"* scenarios to move things along. *"What if we were able to include free delivery for the first 90 days? Would that make a difference, Jim?"*

9. Don't be afraid to walk away. The other party is negotiating with you in the first place because you have something they want. Play this card very carefully. If the other party tries the same tactic on you, consider calling their bluff.

10. Push the deadline. If your homework has uncovered the other party's deadline, use that knowledge. The closer you get to the deadline the more he'll be willing to accept your offer.

11. <u>Make a special offer</u>. Throw in something that won't cost you an arm and a leg, but that might close the transaction. Use this with the *"what if"* game. *"What if you can move in rent-free for 90 days?"*

12. <u>Take one step at a time</u>. Sure, you're climbing a mountain with the words *"closed sale"* at the top. But you get there by taking one small step at a time. Focus on that next step and then the next and the one after. That's how you'll get to the top.

13. <u>Use body language</u>. Use it to express opinions in non-verbal language. Also use it to accurately gauge the other person's attitude.

14. <u>Throw the other party off balance a bit</u>. Offer something *"out of the blue"* to shake things up. An unusual point in the negotiation process might be enough to knock them off the fence of indecision.

15. <u>Don't negotiate with someone who can't approve your proposal</u>. Pretty much anything less than negotiating with the final decision-maker is a waste of time.

16. <u>Give to get</u>. Negotiation is a two-way street. Keep the balance by giving something when you get something.

17. <u>Document your presentation</u>. Remember that a statement not backed up with proof is nothing more than a claim. Document every negotiation point.

18. <u>Counter a negative with a negative</u>. When the other party asks for something you can't or don't want to give, state the negative impact such action would have on you, the other party, and possibly the industry.

19. <u>If practical, allow the other party to take temporary possession of the article being negotiated</u>. For example, if you're selling an automobile, offer to let the prospect

drive it home and keep it over the weekend. Often, once someone is in possession of something, they'll want to hang on to it. This is known as *"The Puppy Dog Close."*

20. When feasible, schedule negotiations according to your internal clock. Some of us are morning people and some of us function best late in the day or even in the evenings. Learn what time of day you are most mentally sharp and set the time for your presentations accordingly as much as possible. Of course, you'll run into buyers who prefer to review presentations at a specific time of day. If that's the case, you may need to defer to their time schedules. Being flexible is one of the most important keys to business.

21. Don't hesitate to call a foul. If the other side takes an unfair advantage or position, go ahead and say so. You don't have to scream or get angry but be firm in pointing it out. Often, the other person will try to make things right by giving in to one or more of your key negotiation points.

22. *"No"* often means *"maybe"* or *"not today"* or *"not that way,"* and *"maybe"* is almost a *"yes."* When you hear those marvelous words, ask questions to get the buyer to get specific about what's holding them back. It could be something you haven't yet covered, or something minor you didn't even think about.

23. Negotiate with deadlines. You have deadlines. The other parties have deadlines. Use them to your best advantage.

24. Take care of yourself. Negotiations can be extremely strenuous. Make certain that you are of sound mind, body and spirit when you begin.

25. Take symbolic control. Take the power seat or power corner in a room. Wear power suits and use symbols of power.

26. <u>Put the agreement in writing</u>. If you don't have approved paperwork, you don't have a sale.
27. <u>Use allies</u>. The more people and organizations on your side the better. They don't have to be physically present in a negotiation. Testimonial letters, videos or audios can be very effective allies.
28. <u>Stay focused</u>. It's easy to get distracted or to be led into distraction by the other side. Use your agenda to stay focused on the task at hand.

These tips and guidelines will help you design, create and benefit from win/win scenarios in all of your negotiations. As we noted earlier, you're already halfway there. Study and practice the techniques in this chapter and you'll soon be all the way home.

SUMMARY

Just as every human interaction is a sales presentation, most involve negotiation points. Decide in advance what is and is not negotiable in every situation. When you know this in advance, you'll be working from a much stronger position.

CHAPTER 9
Building Long Term Relationships with Clients

Our relationships with people are formed by small moments -
and relationships are crucial in business.

– TOM RATH

The opinion of your company, formed by customers, will likely depend on the individual people they encounter within the company—not on your company's overall reputation in the marketplace. The game of getting and keeping happy customers is won or lost on the front lines where the customers come in contact with employees. For most companies, that contact is made by sales, service, and support people. As we covered earlier, the people you hire can make or break your company based on how they handle themselves with clients.

Think about it. When you go into the grocery store and the item you want is out of stock, you ask a clerk about it, right? If the item is out of stock and the clerk doesn't know when it will be available, you don't leave the store upset with the clerk. You leave with the memory of disappointment in the store itself.

If the clerk had provided smart customer service and given you an apology, explanation and/or a due date for the item and a rain check for it, your feelings about the company would be different. You might still be unhappy about not getting the item, but at least you'd feel as though they cared about having your business. Again, it's all on how the clerk handled the situation, isn't it?

In the past, many businesses chalked up dissatisfied customers to the cost of doing business. Today, word of that dissatisfying experience can make it around the world before the customer even makes it home. That's why it's more important than ever to train everyone on your staff how you want your clients treated. Some reports show that average businesses lose between 15 and 25 percent of their clients yearly to poor service. We know you're not aiming to build an *average* business. So, it must be your goal to build long term relationships with your clients.

Business owners must set the stage for how clients are to be treated. With the right strategies in place, each client will refer many others to your business, spurring organic growth. Common themes that run through the customer service departments of today's hottest entrepreneurial success stories are that the businesses really care about their clients—because they do. They have to!

Let Your Clients Do the Bragging

Exceptional service will not only bring you referred business but could even garner positive press for your business. Here are two stories about businesses that went the extra mile and made the news:

$$$

Story #1: Trader Joe's

An 89-year-old man was snowed in at his Pennsylvania home around the holidays, and his daughter was worried that he wasn't going to have access to enough food due to the impending storm and overall bad weather in the area. After calling many grocery stores in a desperate attempt to find someone who would deliver to her father's home, she finally reached someone at Trader Joe's who also told her they do not deliver "under normal circumstances."

Given these extreme circumstances, they told her that they would gladly deliver groceries to her father and even suggested additional items that would fit with his special low-sodium diet. After placing the order, the daughter was told not to worry about the bill. The food would be delivered free of charge. The employee then wished her a Merry Christmas.

Less than 30 minutes later, the food was at the man's doorstep. In refusing to let company policy get in the way of a customer in need, Trader Joe's showed that customer service can simply be about doing the right thing.

Story #2: Ritz-Carlton

Chris Hurn's son left his favorite stuffed giraffe, "Joshie," in their hotel room after a recent stay. Mr. Hurn assured his distraught son that

Joshie was just staying a few extra days on vacation. He then called the staff at the Ritz and relayed the story he had told his son.

In an all-star effort to make everything right for their customer, the staff at the Ritz created a series of photographs that included all the activities Joshie had been involved in during his "extended vacation." Joshie spent time by the pool, helping the staff on the computer, relaxing in the spa, driving a golf cart on the property, and visiting with various staff members before returning home. When Joshie arrived home, included in the shipment were all of the photos of his adventures.

$$\$\$\$$$

Customer service consultant Peter Shankman, says, *"Customer service isn't about telling people how awesome you are. It's about creating stories that do the talking for you."*

Characteristics of Top Customer Service People

When you hire right and nurture an attitude of service among your team members, your business will grow by word-of-mouth. Help your employees understand the value of treating each client as an individual. When people know they're being heard and understood, they're more likely to remain long term clients. And, companies with a high rating for customer service often see as much as a 25 percent increase in sales over their competition.

Here are some qualities you will find in exceptional customer service people.

1. <u>Empathetic</u>. Having empathy means they can see the situation from the other person's perspective.

2. <u>Curious</u>. The best customer service people are curious about every aspect of your product and its use. They can't wait to hear of the latest advances or options, so they can help your clients more effectively.

3. <u>Kind</u>. Kind people will seek out opportunities to make someone else's day.

4. <u>Good listeners</u>. They don't just hear the words delivered by the people who purchase your products, they grasp the meaning and tone of those words.

5. <u>Professional</u>. Even if they never meet clients in person, they walk, talk, dress and act as if they do.

6. <u>Optimistic</u>. They are cheerful and upbeat. Even when faced with customer challenges, they approach those challenges with the attitude that they will overcome them and meet or exceed client expectations.

Be observant of these characteristics in your staff. Give them positive reinforcement when you recognize they are doing their jobs well. You might even hand write notes of thanks for their efforts on behalf of the company. Be sure to share positive comments from customers with your team members as another means of reinforcing the value of the service they provide. We all need recognition every now and then.

Remember, to encourage everyone on the team to use their customer service skills within the organization as well. We all sell ourselves to each person we encounter. Maximize the benefit of the great customer service skills your staff has by encouraging the same excellent service with co-workers.

When and Why to Contact Clients

The business world is not quite as simple as *"you sell, they buy."* While that is the premise of business, succeeding long term requires a lot more engagement than that. It takes time and concerted effort to grow a loyal, long-term following. Don't make the mistake of only contacting clients with sales offers.

Here are some suggestions for other reasons and times to contact clients to make your relationship with them stronger.

1. <u>Say thank you</u>. This is the simplest and one of the most powerful practices that's readily available to every business, no matter how large or small. Send an email, a post card, a formal thank you note, or even call simply to thank your clients for their business. Don't talk about yourself or tell them how big the company has grown. Just offer a simple, *"Thank you for being a valued client."*

2. <u>Provide interesting or valuable information</u>. This could be done in the form of a newsletter or a simple email message. If your business provides automotive care, send a light-read article about industry recommendations for each season. If you sell jewelry, remind clients of how to best care for the pieces they've purchased. If your product is insurance, consider providing information about trends among the various demographic groups you serve.

3. <u>Conduct a survey</u>. Keep surveys short and simple, limiting them to two or three questions that can be answered quickly. Design your surveys to get answers to questions you've been asking yourself.

- *"Your feedback is important to us. Would you find more value in X or Y as a service we might provide in the future?"*
- *"Knowing that you have enjoyed A in the past, is B something you might enjoy in the future?"*
- *"How are we doing? Are we providing the level of value and service you expect?"*

The feedback provided by clients will bring you valuable information regarding any next steps you're thinking about taking with your business.

1. <u>Acknowledge holidays, birthdays, anniversaries and other relevant events.</u> This is where the information you've gathered about your clients comes into play. How nice is it to receive a birthday card a few days early—to get the celebration started? If you're not certain about religious matters, don't risk offending someone. Send a Thanksgiving card or note of positivity for the New Year instead. Instead of following the crowd with sales offers for President's Day, 4th of July, and Labor Day, send non-sales messages pertinent to each holiday. The key is to be different to be remembered!

2. <u>Make random phone calls.</u> Use a Customer Relationship Management (CRM) tool that allows you to schedule contacts with each client. Include every client in this program. Have the team reach out by phone to a certain number of clients each day. Have them thank the client for their business. You should make some of these calls as well. Consider them a random act of kindness. State that you're just checking in to ensure that the client is

still happy with the product or service and ask what the company can do for them. You'll get great feedback. You'll find out if someone is unhappy (and be able to fix it rather than having them tell others about their unhappiness). You'll also get some excellent testimonials.

Helping the Unhappy Client

Too many people, when faced with clients who range from dissatisfied to downright angry, choose the loser's path by postponing handling the situation. Worse yet, they handle it inappropriately. Postponement doesn't make the problem go away. It results in one of two things.

1. The angry client decides the problem isn't worth the aggravation and cools down.
2. The client gets so angry that the next time you hear from him or her is through some sort of official (and possibly legal) notification. Worse yet, you'll see your company named on the local news channel in one of those consumer protection segments.

If you're the business owner, you may think it's okay to lose one client who's unhappy, but it's not. As we've mentioned before, there's that whole social media bullhorn that people use to vent to the world. Can you see how your business could be hurt by that?

Naturally, no one wants to walk into a lion's den and face the angry client. However, you must consider the value of each client to you, your reputation, and the company. In most cases, it will be worth your while to face that angry client and get the situation resolved as quickly as possible.

Here are ten steps for facing and dispelling another person's anger. They work well in most situations mainly because you're giving the client the attention their dissatisfaction deserves. Review them with your staff and give them your parameters for handling various types of situations.

1. <u>Acknowledge the other person's anger quickly</u>. Nothing adds more fuel to a fire than having your anger ignored or belittled. The faster the client's anger is recognized, the better.

2. <u>Make it plain that you're concerned</u>. Tell them you realize just how angry they are. Let them know that you are taking the situation seriously. Make notes of every detail they give you. And let them see you taking those notes.

3. <u>Be patient</u>. Let them get it all out. Never interrupt. In many cases, the best move is to simply listen. They'll wind themselves down eventually. In some cases, they'll realize they blew the situation out of proportion. They are then likely to accept nearly any solution you offer.

4. <u>Keep calm</u>. Most angry people say things they don't really mean. Learn to let those things pass and take them up after you've solved the present challenge — only if you feel it's necessary to do so.

5. <u>Ask questions</u>. Your aim is to discover the specific things that you can do to correct the problem. Try to get specific information about the difficulties the problem has caused, rather than a general venting of hot air.

6. <u>Get them talking about solutions</u>. This is where you will learn just how reasonable this client is. By the time you get to this step, their anger should have cooled enough to discuss the challenge rationally. If it hasn't, suggest

scheduling another time to help them come up with a reasonable solution, even if it's in an hour. Let them do the rest of their fuming on their own time.

7. Agree on a solution. After you know exactly what the challenge is, look for a resolution. Propose something specific. Start with whatever will bring them the best and quickest relief. You may be surprised that some clients will ask for less in terms of a resolution than you had expected to give. They want acknowledgement and restitution—not revenge.

8. Agree on a schedule. Once you've agreed on a solution, set up a schedule for its implementation. Agree to a realistic time frame you know you can handle. The biggest mistake you can make is to agree to something that cannot be done. If you do, you'd better be ready to face another bout of anger when you don't come through.

9. Meet your schedule. Give this schedule top priority. You've talked yourself into a second chance with this client, so make sure you don't blow it.

10. Send a thank you note and check back with them. Thank the client for their patience and understanding as you resolved their challenge. The time frame for follow up will depend on the issue and your type of business but consider checking back with them somewhere between ten days and two weeks after the challenge is resolved to ensure they're still happy with the results.

Once you've satisfied the client regarding this situation, you will have earned another opportunity to serve their needs in the future… and the needs of those they'll tell about how well you handled it.

How You Say What You Say

There's an adage that goes like this, *"It's not what you say, but how you say it that matters."* In business, what you say *and* how you say it both matter. When you or your team members engage in conversation with anyone while representing the company, suggest that they use the term *"we"* instead of *"I."* The *"we"* we're referring to is *"we, the company."* This is a subtle thing but effective in building an image of a team of people serving the client's individual needs.

Encourage your team to replace the phrase, *"I don't know"* with *"I'll find out"* or *"I'll be happy to look into that for you."* Such phrases lend a more service-oriented mindset to the conversation.

Two of the most important words to use when communicating with others are *"I understand."* In Susan Cain's book, *Quiet Power,* she says, *"People don't buy because they understand. They buy because they feel understood."* When you can demonstrate to someone that you truly understand their wants, needs, and concerns, they'll relax with you and be more open in all your communications with them. When you say, *"I understand,"* or *"Help me to understand,"* you're communicating that you're on their side. You're dedicated to service.

Two more good words to add to everyone's vocabulary are *"flexible"* and *"feasible."* These are especially useful when a client challenges something in company policy. They help you avoid having the client feel confronted when the response is not what they want to hear. *"We like to be flexible to accommodate the special needs of our clients. I'm happy to look into what might be a feasible response to your request."*

When you encounter a particularly chatty client, and believe us, it will happen, use these words to get off the call, *"Just one more thing, Mrs. Sadler, before we wrap up our call…"* You would then either ask a yes/no question or confirm that you've taken care of the need they had when the call began. It's a courteous way of saying, *"I've got to move on to something else."*

Listening Skills

We each have two ears and one mouth. That's the proportion with which they should be used to achieve success in business… and in personal relationships. Strive to listen twice as much as you speak, and you'll be amazed at what you learn. You see, when you're talking, you're only covering what you already know. When you listen, you're gaining new knowledge or a new perspective on the subject.

There are some common listening distractions found in business situations that we advise you to work on eliminating.

1. Music – While having music playing in the background might prove positive or uplifting for the staff members, it could be distracting while on a call with a client. Keep the music but make a call to each member of the team to hear how loud it is in the background. Adjust the volume if necessary.

2. Fatigue. When we're tired, we just don't listen well. If possible, note the best times of day for each team member with regard to their energy. Some people are morning-people. Others have more energy after lunch. Take advantage of that energy when it comes to the most important calls of the day. Granted, you want to make

calls when it's most convenient for clients, but if there's some flexibility, have your people take advantage of their own energy levels as well.

3. <u>Too much stuff within sight.</u> This includes too many files or folders on a computer screen and too many things on a desk. When other business is within sight, there's a high possibility that your team member's mind may wander during client calls. Help your people develop effective strategies for allowing them to focus on whatever task is at hand. When you help them to do the most productive thing possible at every given moment, everyone wins.

4. <u>Work overload.</u> When you're growing, it's normal that people will be asked to progressively take on more work. Encourage your team members to be open about how much they can handle. When we have multiple projects under way, it's easy to have a detail about one of them pop up at the most inconvenient time, such as when speaking with a client about something else.

When you and your team members adopt attitudes of service where your goal is to make the other person's day/week/life better for having spoken with you, you'll be a long way toward developing those long-term client relationships that you're dreaming of.

SUMMARY

Awareness is the key to developing professional customer service skills. Once you and your team members or staff are aware of the various strategies in this chapter, you'll create effective policies for how to handle each type of situation—to the benefit of all.

CHAPTER 10

When Things Don't Go as Planned

"Never give up because you failed once or twice, know that failure is sometimes the universe telling you that your mission in life is somewhere else."

–JACK MA, CREATOR OF ALIBABA

It's important to remain open and flexible to succeed as an entrepreneur. There will be days, weeks, or possibly months when business just doesn't go as planned. When you adopt a mindset of learning from every experience, all the little detours you're likely to encounter will be less painful than if your plan is rigid or if your attitude is: *"It's my way, or the highway."*

When you start a business, and let's say you're a solopreneur, how things are done is always up to you. You get to make all the decisions. You get to determine the quality of your work. And, you get to speak directly with buyers and clients. You are the king or queen of your world. You are also the chimney sweep, cook, and janitor. When you're first getting your bearings in the marketplace that's all well and good. It's important for you to be the front-line person to see firsthand the reactions people have to your product. There are certain lessons of business that are best learned firsthand.

When your business grows, and you simply cannot physically or mentally do it all, you'll have to depend on others. Those others will never feel the same way about your baby—your startup. They'll never treat it with the same tender, loving care that you've given it—because it's not their baby. Therefore, even when you hire people with incredible talent and skills, something is bound to go awry.

When Challenges Arise

What matters is how you handle those situations. Do you:

1. Blow up, letting your blood pressure go through the roof, and berate the offending parties?
2. Beat yourself up mentally for not being more involved? Or for hiring incompetent people (even though five minutes ago you felt they were highly competent)?
3. Dwell on the error, allowing old Mr. Fear to creep into your mind and body, taking you into a downward spiral where your confidence takes a hit?

Those are the three most likely negative scenarios. Number one is the least healthy choice with regard to your physical wellbeing. Trust us. Nothing—absolutely nothing—is worth affecting your bodily health. We've heard stories of people punching walls in anger, throwing things, and storming out of meetings. Those actions do no one involved any good. Well, maybe if you storm out of the meeting and keep walking until you calm down, can think rationally, and humble yourself to apologize for your actions, storming out might be a temporary solution. It's not, however, the way to handle challenges on a regular basis.

Neither is it healthy to beat yourself up mentally. Ok. Go ahead and wallow in the misery of the moment—but only for a moment. Get that out of your system as fast as possible and move on to solution mode. What can be done to resolve the situation? How can the challenge be overcome and prevented in the future?

Once the situation is resolved—even if it's a temporary solution—take a moment to value the lesson that was learned from the experience. Maybe your people aren't incompetent. That would be a generalization. Maybe they were just not skilled *enough* to deal with that situation. Help them learn how to handle things better the next time—in case there is one. Then, let everyone get back to work.

Dwelling on the mistake does nothing more than keep you in the past—even if the past was 15 minutes ago. As a business owner, it's important to stay focused in the present and plan for the future. The past can't help you move forward other than learning lessons from it as we already mentioned.

Do Like the Boy Scouts and Be Prepared

The way to handle challenges is to prepare for them. You do that by envisioning potential scenarios and figuring out how you'd deal with them. Practice creating a "what if" list every now and then.

- What if the shipment of inventory is delayed by a week?
- What if John, Ashley, and Sara all need to be away from the business at the same time?
- What if I have a flat tire on the way to the next big client presentation?
- What if the computer system goes down?

The point of this exercise is not to freak you out or to depress you with all the negative things that could happen. It's to help you think ahead so you can *respond* instead of reacting to those types of situations.

Take a lesson from the world of Zen teachings. Even though the dictionary uses the terms *react* and *respond* in a similar manner, what happens with each is very different. When you *react*, your actions tend to be defensive. The challenge has come at you as a combatant. You go into warrior mode. To *respond* requires that brief little pause where you are thoughtful about the challenge. *Response* involves reasoning. It comes more from logical thought than emotion.

Think about it. Police and firefighters are called out to all sorts of challenging situations. They're not called *first reactors*, are they? No. They're *first responders*. They train constantly for all different types of scenarios. If you were in a wreck, you wouldn't want the guy with the "jaws of life" to say, *"I've never cut a car door off before, but I'm sure this equipment can handle it."* No! You want someone who has not only used that equipment but did so safely and effectively. You want someone with a "best practices" level of knowledge and skill. That's what you'll build by playing the "what if" game with your business.

Understanding that point, let's consider the bullet points above. How would you respond to a delayed shipment? You'd probably start by determining exactly how long the current inventory will last. Hopefully, the person handling purchasing allowed for that when placing the order. If you find out that you are going to run out and that orders will be delayed, how will you address that with buyers? Do you email them about the delay? Call them? Who would be responsible for making those contacts? What would you want them to say? Would you offer the buyers a little something extra for the inconvenience? Would you ship the product to them via a faster method? If so, what would that cost the business in revenue versus the goodwill it will create? When you think through the answers to those questions, you'll realize a lot of things about your business. We hope you'll be pleasantly surprised with the strategies that come to mind.

Let's move on to the next bullet. Three of your key employees all have very good reasons for needing to be elsewhere on the same day. You may have to set aside your business owner hat and jump in to handle their most important duties. You may be able to schedule time to cross train someone else to help with those duties. You may want to re-prioritize everyone's work load temporarily to just get the critical tasks done. If you have plenty of notice, perhaps some of the prep work for that day's requirements can be done in advance. Or, maybe a deadline can be moved. There's that flexibility thing again.

Flat tire on your way to an important meeting? Have the numbers for taxi services and car services in your phone, along with the apps for *Uber* and *Lyft*. Don't assume you'll never need these. One occurrence of a major transportation delay is worth this preparation. Don't assume just one option will do. You'll want to reach whoever can get you to fastest. You'll also want the numbers for the people you're meeting with. And, consider having a friend, or other team member pop out to handle your vehicle situation so you can keep your appointment. If you live in a big city, having an app with the subway or bus schedule on your phone could bring you another viable option for continuing to your destination.

How about that darn computer system? Technological challenges can be super frustrating. We depend so much on technology. Hopefully, your most important information is cloud-based so you can access it from anywhere. A low-tech solution would be to print out the details of the next day's schedule at the end of each day. Or, at least take a photo on your phone of the information you need the most.

Build the skills you need to be a responder instead of a reactor. When those inevitable challenges arise, you'll avoid a lot of the physical and mental frustration experienced by those who don't prepare.

$$$

Don't Rain on Your Sunny Side

There's an old bluegrass song called *Keep on the Sunny Side*. One of the stanzas could have been written about the challenges entrepreneurs face.

Tho storm and its fury broke today
Crushing hopes that we cherish so dear
Clouds and storms will in time pass away
And the sun again will shine bright and clear

They chorus reminds us to *"Keep on the sunny side, always on the sunny side. Keep on the sunny side of life."* And that simple country wisdom is some of the best advice you will ever get. The life of an entrepreneur is one of constant challenge and it's easy to slip into negative thinking. Negative thinking starts the entrepreneur on a mental and emotional downward spiral. If not corrected, that downward movement will inevitably damage or even ruin the business. Beyond that, many lives and even entire families have been damaged by the loss of a business.

Negative thinking is dangerous territory, especially for someone putting everything on the line. Remember, we humans aren't wired for the sunny side – most of us anyway. For some reason we're drawn to the negative impulses of human natures. That thinking may date back to our caveman days when we sat around the campfire knowing that the human being is not at the top of the food chain. Somehow, even today, our minds seem to be reminding us that there are things *"out there"* with fangs and claws just licking their lips and waiting to pounce when we let our guard down. With all that heritage going against us, how do we fight back? How do we overcome our negative thoughts? And how do we get back on and remain on "the sunny side" of life?

We recommend three steps. They're easy to understand and just as easy to follow. The key is to implement them the moment that you recognize a negative thought entering your mind.

Three Steps to Having Your Life "Sunny Side Up"

Step One: Recognize the challenge. Something bad has happened, is about to happen, or you think it might be about to happen. Negative impulses have rushed in and are even now trying to stifle your efforts to stay positive. Don't dwell on those negative impulses. Put them out of your mind. Or at least, shove them to the back of your mind where they can't be seen.

In a way, our attraction to the negative side of life is something of an addiction. As with any addiction, you can't cure the problem until you recognize it. Realizing you have allowed what the *Star Wars* crowd might call "the dark side" intrude into your life isn't the end of things. It's the beginning of getting back to where you belong.

Step Two: Eliminate those negative thoughts immediately and ruthlessly. As they say in the spy movies, *"Terminate with extreme prejudice."* There is just no room in the life of a successful entrepreneur for negative thinking. It's like a virus. If left untreated it will spread throughout the entire system. In the world of business that system includes you and your entire organization. There's just too much at stake here. When you feel that negativity coming on, take action against it without hesitation.

Step Three: Replace the negative with a positive. For purposes of illustration, let's assume you are about to make a major presentation to a new potential client. Without warning, the image of that prospect spitting out a definitive *"no"* to your proposal slips into your mind. Recognize it. Kill it. And then visualize that same prospect saying *"yes."* When we say visualize, we mean really visualize. Don't just see a picture of someone nodding in approval. Drink it in. Feel the warmth in the client's acceptance and in his or her handshake after the presentation. Hear the delight in the new client's voice when he realizes you've just solved a major challenge for them. Feel the pen in your hand as you both approve the paperwork, work order or agreement. Use all your senses to build a full sensory view of a successful meeting.

We Attract Who We Are

The makers of the cleaning product *Formula 409* state that the name reflects the number of the formulated cleanser that finally met all their needs for a successful product. Think about that for a moment. *Formula 409's* success is built on 408 failures! What if they had given up at formula 408? It's like the old joke about the man who failed at inventing a new lemon-lime soft drink called *Six Up*. He never knew how close he came to achieving great success.

The move from fighting with negative thoughts into the arena of success built on positive thought and action starts within you—within your mind and in your ability to control your thoughts, channel them in the right direction, and act accordingly. Recognize that the modern world constantly assaults that sunny side of life. We get it in our reading/viewing/listening to the daily news, from our friends and associates, on social media, and even the members of our families. Being confronted with negativity is unavoidable. Giving in to it is another matter and it's a matter of choice.

Realize that nothing is forcing you to adopt and live in a negative state of mind. You can change your way of thinking, your position in whatever circumstances you find yourself, your place in the grand scheme of things, simply by controlling your thoughts.

Action follows thought. That is an undeniable fact of life. It's a fundamental law of the universe. We have encountered far too many business people who thought themselves into failure, even into bankruptcy. It starts with buying into bad news or negative ideas and feeding that perspective with self-talk that supports it. *"The economy is bad. I can't survive this."* That thought gets embedded, like a virus it spreads, and in an amazingly short amount of time self-thought becomes that self-fulfilling prophesy. The business doesn't survive.

It doesn't have to be that way. It shouldn't be that way. Any time a negative image strikes, replace it with a positive one—immediately.

Another fundamental law of the universe is the law of attraction. Like attracts like. If you think bad things are going to happen they will. Your subconscious mind acts to make your conscious thoughts real. Remember, the subconscious mind doesn't make judgements – it just does what it's told. Feed it images of failure and it will do everything possible to make those thoughts come to be. Feed it positive images and it will kick into gear and start turning *those* images into reality.

Control your thinking. We don't attract what we want; we attract what we think and what we are. This isn't a new concept. In the *King James* version of the *Bible* we read *Proverbs 23:7* which says, *"For as he thinketh in his heart, so is he."* We would like to add a post script to that verse and note that what we think is *what we bring about*. The focus of our thoughts becomes the focus and eventually the reality of our lives.

Plain and simple, ultimately success as an entrepreneur it is a matter of choice. What choice are you prepared to make?

$$$

What Did You Do Right?

It's all too common that when things don't go as planned to have people question themselves. Unfortunately, the first question is usually, *"What did I do wrong?"* We highly recommend turning that phrase around right now and forever. Whenever things don't go your way, ask yourself, *"What did I do right?"* When you start from a positive viewpoint, something happens in your brain. Instead of beating yourself up about what you could have done differently, you come from a position of success in that you did a bunch of things right before the challenge occurred. This strategy has been known to improve not only your attitude about what happened, but the quality of the lessons learned or strategies for overcoming challenges.

Too many people will focus heavily on the one bad thing that happened rather than on the 100 or more good things. It's a sad way to live, but it's how many of us have been raised to react to situations. Let's say you heard a big, fat *"no"* from a potential client—one that you've been wooing for some time. What did you do right? Here's a short list:

- You performed your job of prospecting for new business.
- You made an initial contact with the potential client and persuaded them to consider your offering.
- You got out of bed and to the meeting at the appointed time.
- You delivered what you believed to be a solid presentation based on the information you had about the client's needs.

You may even have prepared to address anticipated concerns and created a list of potential negotiation points. Don't you feel better seeing that list than just beating yourself up about a lost sale? When something goes wrong, learn from it and move on. Maybe what went wrong wasn't even within your power to control. Maybe the buyer had a bad day or a bad experience with another salesperson who came in ahead of you. Never assume that the *"no"* is your fault unless and until you learn that directly from the client. Wondering how to do that? Read on.

Dead Sale Autopsy

We will admit that the following strategy takes some guts to pull off. However, you've demonstrated that you have no shortage of guts by starting your own business. When, after much and great preparation, you don't close a sale, invest a bit of time in analyzing what it was that negatively impacted the sale, so you learn the lessons from the situation.

Hopefully, you would have used the *Lost Sale Close* from chapter 7 to find out directly from the client why they didn't go ahead. If you didn't, there were likely some other signs throughout your presentation when you realized the situation was getting away from you. Invest 10 to 15 minutes running the presentation over in your mind until you sense that moment. Let the lessons learned from lost sales become stepping stones instead of stumbling blocks. Acquire enough stepping stones and you can build a bridge to a higher level of professionalism.

The most common points to learn from dead sale autopsies is when and where there was a breakdown in communication; or whether the client's expectations about money or value were inconsistent with your offer. Those are the most common ones, but you won't know for certain unless you investigate.

If you really can't come up with any reasons why the buyer didn't go ahead, consider giving them a call in the next day or so after getting the *"no."* Say something to this effect, *"Bill, I know you decided to go with another company for your (name your product). I just want to thank you for the time you spent considering my product. May I just ask you a few quick questions to be 100% clear on why you made your decision? What were the main benefits that made you choose the other company? Is there anything I could have done better in my presentation that may have swayed your decision more favorably? Please give me your honest answers. Don't worry about hurting my ego. I'm a business person. I want to learn how we might do a better job in the marketplace. It's my goal to learn as much as possible from each presentation—sale or no sale. I'm sure your company would like to gain the same kind of information on sales not made, right?"*

Most people are good and nice. They like to give help when help is needed or asked for. With this strategy you can learn so much. And, if they say *"no"* again, you've lost nothing. The sale was already gone. You've simply created an opportunity to demonstrate your level of professionalism.

If you do gain valuable input from this conversation, be sure to send that decision-maker a thank you note and perhaps a little gift—if it's appropriate within your industry.

SUMMARY

Developing long-term clients works a lot like developing long-term friendships. Sincerely care about your clients' satisfaction with the product. Ask for and listen to their feedback. Handle challenges promptly and effectively. Going the extra mile with service doesn't cost much money. It just takes a bit of effort. The goodwill it generates can mean the difference between being an average company and becoming a great one.

ABOUT THE AUTHORS

Tom Hopkins

Tom Hopkins is recognized throughout the world as America's #1 Sales trainer. He has taught, motivated and inspired over five million individuals directly through his seminars, and as a consultant to some of the most prominent companies and organizations in the world. His books, audios and videos have sold in the millions. His books include the 1.6 million-selling *How to Master the Art of Selling* and *Low Profile Selling*. Other popular titles include *Selling for Dummies,* and *When Buyers Say No.*

Tom's real-world training began in the arena of real estate in the early 1960s. During his first six months, he made one sale making his average earnings only $42 a month. After realizing that selling was a learned skill, he invested his last $150 of savings in a sales training seminar that literally changed his life.

After becoming a dedicated student of the profession of selling and applying what he learned, Tom Hopkins sold more than $1 million worth of $25,000 homes. During his real estate career, he had a total 1,553 of closed property transactions. 365 of them were in a single year! At age 21 he won the Los Angeles Sales and Marketing Institute's coveted *SAMMY* award and by the age of 27 he was a self-made millionaire. Hopkins was then promoted to management in real estate. Under his guidance, his team soon became #1 in their company.

Tom Hopkins' love of teaching others inspired him to launch his own training company in 1976, conducting seminars throughout the United States. The popularity of his proven-effective, basic selling skills training has since taken him to Canada, Europe, Australia, New Zealand, South Africa, the Philippines, Singapore, Malaysia, Vietnam and China.

He is a member of the National Speakers Association and one of its few members to receive its Council of Peers Award for Excellence (CPAE). He has also been recognized with a Lifetime Achievement Award from the National Academy of Best-Selling Authors.

Tom continues to make his training available through seminars, webinars, online courses, books and audio recordings. His specialty is customizing his selling skills for corporate client companies.

Tom Hopkins International, Inc. | 800-528-0446 | www.TomHopkins.com | tomh@tomhopkins.com

Omar Periu

Omar Periu proudly wears his rags to riches story for others to learn from. He went from making $147 a month at age 21 as a personal trainer to multi-millionaire status by age 31. He & his family fled Castro's regime when he was only seven; they arrived in Miami with no money, no family or friends in America & nothing but what they were wearing.

Enduring the taunting of other children, the cold winters of Illinois & the obstacle of language barriers, Omar didn't let it embitter him. Instead, he made the most of his situation. His father, reading from a tattered Spanish copy of Dale Carnegie's book, *"How to Win Friends & Influence People"*, taught Omar an important life lesson. *"It doesn't matter who you are, where you're from or what color you are, you can do anything you put your mind to."*

Omar sought out and studied the masters; he observed the differences between the performance of top achievers and those barely squeaking by. From there, Omar developed his *Zero to Wealth Systems*™, *The Investigative Selling Principles*™, *The One Minute Meeting Effective Presentation System*™, and *From Management to Leadership*™ programs.

Omar's content is fresh and inspiring, his presentations impeccable and his story unforgettable. He is a world-traveled speaker who has spent over two decades educating entrepreneurs, salespeople, and leaders worldwide. He's personally delivered more than 5,000 seminars, and training programs. He has trained more than two million people in more than two-thirds of the Fortune 500 companies; and he has been a featured speaker at events with superstars like Zig Ziglar, General Colin Powell, Larry Bird, Jim

Rohn, Terry Bradshaw, Larry King, Tony Robbins, Don Shula, Lou Holtz, and many more. Omar is a member of the *National Speakers Association* and has been inducted into the prestigious *International Platform Association*.

His articles are published in *SUCCESS Magazine, Sales & Management Magazine, Selling Power Magazine, Martial Arts Success Magazine,* and more. He has authored bestselling books including *Get Fired Up* which hit #3 on Amazon!

Omar has received the *Business Man of the Year* award for the state of Florida, by the Florida Business Advisory Council and is on the Board of Directors to *Wayne Huizenga's School of Entrepreneurs* as well as *Nova Southeastern University.*

Omar has dedicated himself to helping others fulfill their dreams by teaching them how to achieve greatness! Omar helps people build a better self, team and company with a fresh take on age-old solutions. He specifically teaches how to set and achieve goals while ensuring constant and never-ending improvement. More than a motivator, his peers refer to him as *The Master Motivational Teacher.* Omar brings audiences to their feet with his indescribable quality of magnetism.

Omar is available for speaking, training, consulting, and coaching.

Omar Periu International, Inc. | 470-777-2074 | www.OmarPeriu.com | Omar@omarperiu.com

Morgan James
Speakers Group

↗ www.TheMorganJamesSpeakersGroup.com

We connect Morgan James published
authors with live and online events
and audiences who will benefit
from their expertise.

Morgan James makes all of our titles available
through the Library for All Charity Organization.

www.LibraryForAll.org

CPSIA information can be obtained
at www.ICGtesting.com
Printed in the USA
BVHW071055080219
539812BV00003B/136/P